'It opens up a whole new vista of understanding for all who are ready to learn lessons from the past in order to prepare for the future.'

CLIVE CALVER

'Every student of early church history should have a copy! After this, no one could ever call church history boring again.'

BARRY CHANT, Tabor College, Sydney

'Josephine Laffin has written the type of book that anybody who has taught church history . . . will especially appreciate. [It] will provide students with a relatively painless way to learn a good deal of early church history as well as something about the kinds of students they are likely to meet in their seminars.'

RUDOLPH HEINZE, Oak Hill College

D0542396

Josephine Laffin graduated from the University of Adelaide in 1990 with an MA in history. She is currently Church History lecturer for the Flinders University of South Australia and the Adelaide College of Divinity.

# The Duffer's Guide to the Early Church

## THE TUTORIAL NOTES OF MICHAEL ALEXANDER

Josephine Laffin
with a Foreword by Adrian Plass

Marshall Pickering
*An Imprint of* HarperCollins*Publishers*

Marshall Pickering is an Imprint of
HarperCollins*Religious*
Part of HarperCollins*Publishers*
77–85 Fulham Palace Road, London W6 8JB

First published in Australia in 1993
by Openbook Publishers
First published in Great Britain
in 1995 by Marshall Pickering

3   5   7   9   10   8   6   4   2

Josephine Laffin asserts the moral right to be
identified as the author of this work

A catalogue record for this book is
available from the British Library

ISBN 0 551 02914-5

Typeset by Harper Phototypesetters Limited
Northampton, England
Printed and bound in Great Britain by
HarperCollinsManufacturing Glasgow

# Acknowledgements

The author would like to thank the Rev. Drs Guy Hartcher CM, Brian Jackson CM, and Duncan Reid, lecturers in early church history, for employing her to conduct tutorials; students who contributed to lively discussions; and, above all, her parents and sister for their continued love, support and encouragement.

Thanks are also due to the following for permission to quote copyright material:

B. T. Batsford Ltd, London, for the quotation from Epiphanius in Stephen Benko, *Pagan Rome and the Early Christians*, 1985, p. 65.

Darton Longman & Todd Ltd, London, for the quotation from W. H. C. Frend, *The Rise of Christianity*, 1984, p. 328.

Liturgical Press, Michael Glazier Section, Collegeville, Minnesota, for quotations from the letters of Ignatius and the *Didoche* in Joseph Lienhard, *Ministry* (Message of the Fathers of the Church, no. 8), 1984, p. 29, 32, 35; for the quotation from Elizabeth Clark, *Women in the Early Church* (Message of the Fathers of the Church, no. 13), 1983, p. 15; for the quotation from *Against Heresies* by Irenaeus in Robert Eno, *Teaching Authority in the Early Church* (Message of the Fathers of the Church, no. 14), 1984, p. 43; for quotations from Justin Martyr, Tertullian's *Against the Jews*, and Origen in Louis Swift, *The Early Fathers on War and Military Service* (Message of the Fathers of the Church, no. 19), 1983, p. 18; for quotations from John Chrysostom in Peter Phan, *Social Thought* (Message of The Fathers of the Church, no. 20), 1984, pp. 152-3, 158-9.

Paulist Press, New York, for the quotation from Raymond Brown and John Meier, *Antioch and Rome: New Testament Cradles of Catholic Christianity*, 1983, pp. 2–6; and for the quotation from Athanasius, *The Life of Antony and the Letter to Marcellinus*, translation and Introduction by Robert Gregg, Classics of Western Spirituality, 1980, pp. 38–9.

Penguin Books Ltd, London, for the quotation from Ignatius's letter to Polycarp in M. Stanniforth ed., *Early Christian Writings*, 1968, p. 127.

SCM Press Ltd, London, for quotations from Irenaeuss in C. Richardson ed., *Early Christian Fathers*, Library of Christian Classics, vol 1, 1953, pp. 363–4; and for the quotation from Arius's *Thalia* in Jean Comby, *How to Read Church History*, Vol. 1: *From the Beginnings to the Fifteenth Century*, translated by John Bowden and Margaret Lydamore, 1985, p. 89.

SPCK, London, for quotations from St Ambrose and the formula agreed to between Cyril of Alexandria and John of Antioch in J. Stevenson ed., *Creeds, Councils and Controversies: Documents Illustrative of the History of the Church AD 337–461*, revised with additional documents by W. H. C Frend, 1989, pp. 128, 314–15; for quotations from the account of the martyrs of Lyons and Vienne, Origen on war, and the Nicene Creed in J. Stevenson ed., *A New Eusebius, Documents Illustrating the History of the Church to AD 337*, new edition revised by W. H. C. Frend, 1987, pp. 36–42, 94, 99.

Thames and Hudson International Ltd, London, for the quotation from Peter Brown, *The World of Late Antiquity*, 1971, p. 110.

William B. Eerdmans Publishing Co., Grand Rapids, Michigan, for quotations from Minucius Felix, Lucian, and the author in Everett Ferguson, *Backgrounds of Early Christianity*, 1987, pp. 475, 477, 489.

# Contents

# Foreword

I am frequently appalled by my own ignorance. All I know of theology is that it is an anagram of 'O, get holy!' I can't spell exegesis without a dictionary – let alone do it. My preaching invariably fails because I can never think of three note-headings beginning with the same letter. As for church history, I can hardly remember last Sunday's sermon. The rest is a fog.

Sometimes I have tried to educate and enlighten myself in these areas, but I never get very far. The books I borrow or steal (same thing) are full of great, opaque slabs of sonorous prose. I labour miserably for a while, but the sheer lack of humanity in most of these worthy tomes means that they never touch me on any real level, and I give up.

Josephine Laffin must have read those same books, because she has created a way for people like me to actually enjoy absorbing information, by placing it in the context of real people with real personalities and prejudices who are trying to match faith and facts in their own lives.

With wit, warmth and profound understanding she has demonstrated the relevance and importance of historical perspectives to the issues of today.

Michael, Kirsty, Maureen, Christobel, Ruth, Frank, Wade and Neville – the members of the tutorial group – represent all of us in our various attitudes and biases, at times with humour that made me laugh out loud. What a blessing laughter is! I shall never forget Christobel's question-and-answer session on the place of women in the early Church.

I can think of no better book to put in the hands of those who are considering studying early church history, are actually studying it now, or are simply wanting a good, humorous, stimulating read.

I might even have another look at that sonorous prose . . .

Adrian Plass

# WEEK·ONE

## Why study church history anyway?

First tutorial meeting today. Eight people in my group (including me) plus Derek, our tutor. He seems nice, in a quiet sort of way. General introductions and then Derek asked the question: 'Why have you decided to study church history?'

Dead silence.

Eventually Kirsty spoke up. She's a nice-looking kid, dressed in jeans and a jumper, with her hair in a ponytail. She confessed that it was her first year at university and she'd just moved to the city from the country. Was feeling a bit lonely and intimidated by it all. Was really pleased to discover that she could pick up some Theology Department subjects as part of her Bachelor of Arts degree. She thought that it would be nice to meet some Christians. (She belonged to the Baptist youth group at home.)

Thought Derek looked a bit flustered.

Maureen then confided that she was studying church history because her counsellor had advised her to.

Derek looked even more flustered.

I was a bit surprised myself, but Maureen went on to explain that she's in the middle of a divorce and her counsellor recommended that she take up a hobby. She always wanted to go to university but never had the chance before, being a good wife and mother who worked at the school canteen. Now, however, her children have grown up and left home and her husband has walked out too. After extensive therapy Maureen has decided to Take Charge Of Her Life. Step one is enrolling in this course. She thought that she'd start off with an easy subject like history to see whether she could cope with university or not. (She believes in God but doesn't go to church every week.)

'Bravo!' said Christobel encouragingly.

Christobel looks awfully smart and trendy. She has the highest heels on her sandals that I have ever seen and earrings that dangle down to her shoulders. She said that she'd just finished all the available theology subjects (which she absolutely adored) and she felt sure that she would absolutely adore church history too. She then announced, with a provocative smile, that she intended to become the first female Anglican archbishop.

More silence.

Finally Derek looked appealingly at Ruth. She's an older lady with a lovely, gentle smile. She was wearing a plain dress with a little brooch shaped like a cross on her lapel.

'Well, I have always been interested in history,' she said quietly, 'and Christianity seems to me to be a historical religion. The Bible gives an account of God's intervention in the affairs of humanity from the creation of the world to the beginning of the Christian Church. If you don't think he stopped then, it should be useful to continue studying from the point where the New Testament finishes. Most of all, I suppose, I really want to learn more about the origins and development of Christian doctrines and traditions.'

'That is certainly a good reason for taking this course', responded Derek eagerly. 'And I hope that you will all not only learn about the development of traditions but also consider issues that can . . . er . . . confront Christians of all generations. Er . . . things like persecution. We might live in a fairly tolerant Western country but there are still places in the world where Christians . . . er . . . experience considerable hostility.'

We all nodded earnestly.

'I've never studied any history before, and I'm only here now because I'm beginning my Bachelor of Theology degree and Early Church History is a compulsory BTh subject', said Frank frankly. 'But what I want to get from this course is more evidence to use when I'm bringing people to Christ. Because, when the chips are down, that is the only thing that really matters!'

Frank gave a pleased smile.

Wade, however, raised his eyebrows incredulously.

'You can't approach history like that', he stuttered. ' "Bringing people to Christ" is a faith statement. We're here to study history, not faith! What I want to find out is what was *really* going on in the first centuries of the Church. What were *ordinary* people doing in the Roman Empire? What social, economic and political forces shaped Christianity and made it what it is today? And how can we rescue true Christianity from each successive generation's prejudices and misguided tack-ons?'

Christobel absolutely agreed.

Derek then faltered that it might be appropriate at this point to consider another question he wanted to put to us: 'Is it possible to study history objectively?'

'Of course', replied Wade at once. 'It is vital, really vital, that we move beyond the restrictions of faith and find out about *real* people, *real* events, and *real* socio-economic conditions.'

Christobel absolutely agreed again.

'God gave us a brain. She meant us to use it. I approach everything objectively. I question everything. I even,' she added daringly, 'question God!'

Frank looked torn between shock and pity but made a quick recovery.

'No Christian should be afraid to seek the truth, for the ultimate truth is Jesus. As he said himself, John 14:6: "I am the way and the truth and the life. No one comes to the Father except through me." Praise the Lord!'

Wade snorted contemptuously.

'That's just according to the fourth gospel. Few theologians would take that kind of statement seriously today.'

A zealous gleam came into Frank's eyes, but before he could reply Derek hurriedly intervened.

'The main point I . . . er . . . wanted to make when I asked you to consider the issue of objectivity in history is that historians today really feel that it is not possible to be . . . er . . . totally objective. I am not saying that you should not *try* to approach historical study objectively, but that you should be aware that all kinds of things can influence your . . . er . . . interpretation of history. Things like your social, political, religious and educational backgrounds, and so on. Er . . . take George Bush and Saddam Hussein, for instance. If they both wrote an account of the 1990-91 Gulf War, their perspectives would tend to be . . . er . . . slightly different.'

There were polite smiles, but Christobel refused to be put off.

'That's an extreme example. A trained historian writing in fifty years' time would surely be able to look back at the events of the war far more objectively than the main protagonists.'

'Er . . . yes, but his or her religious or political beliefs could still intrude. And one of the great problems he (or she) would face would be the sheer amount of data he (or she) could use, if it could be obtained. It would be humanly impossible to give a really thorough account of absolutely everything that ... er ... took place in the war. What we call "facts" in history are usually the products of ... er ... a process of selection and interpretation. Put another way, E H Carr concludes in his little book *What is History?* that history is ... er ...' (Derek looked at his notes) ' "a continuous process of interaction between the historian and his facts, an unending dialogue between the present and the past".'

'I suppose that when we study the first centuries of the Church we are faced with the opposite problem to too much evidence', remarked Ruth. 'Unfortunately so much has been lost.'

'And what has survived has survived mainly because it was preserved in sexist, elitist monasteries, and bolstered up the monks' particular worldview', added Christobel, doing a sudden about-face. 'Tragically, we have so little left that relates to at least 50 per cent of society: women!'

'That is our great challenge,' cried Wade passionately, 'to find out what was really going on among the marginalized!'

Derek, looking rather harassed, pointed out that we were running out of time, and perhaps we had better decide who wanted to take what tutorial topics. As part of the assessment for the course, everyone has to lead one tutorial.

Christobel immediately asked if she could take week 8 ('How do you account for the role of women in the early Church?'). Wade then said that he'd like to do week 13 ('What provoked John Chrysostom's preaching on social issues and what was its result?'). Frank seized on week 11 ('Discuss the origins of and the debate about whether Jesus was to be understood as God or godly'). Maureen said that she didn't mind what topic she did so long as it wasn't in January, when her daughter was getting married. She eventually decided to have a go at martyrdom in week 5. Neville (who, like me, hadn't said a word during the whole tutorial) offered to do the one on Hellenistic culture, 'to get it over and done with between essays'. Ruth said that she wouldn't mind taking 'The structure and organization of the Church' next week, if no one else wanted to. Kirsty, looking perplexed, asked Derek which of the remaining topics was the least complicated. He suggested that she try the one on persecution, and she shuddered but agreed. That just left me.

I sent up a quick prayer for guidance, opened my eyes and blurted out the first topic I saw: 'Discuss the orthodoxy of Nestorius and the effects on the contemporary christological debates of Cyril's twelve anathematisms'. Heaven knows what it's about, but at least it's not until week 12, so I will have plenty of time to prepare.

That over and done with, everyone got up to leave.

Frank stopped me on the way out and asked in a whisper if I knew whether Derek was a Christian.

I said that I thought that he might be Roman Catholic.

'Yes,' said Frank, 'but is he a Christian?' ???

# Week·Two

## What were the Christians up to?

Today we were supposed to consider the structure and organization of the early Church as revealed in some of the earliest Christian documents outside the New Testament: the *Didache* (Greek for 'teaching') and the letters of Ignatius.

The lecturer advised us last week to remember the 'four Ws' when examining a historical text: Who wrote it? When was it written? Where? And why?

To prepare for the tutorial I read as much as I could find about the *Didache*.

Who wrote it?

Unknown.

When was it written?

Unknown.

Where was it written?

Unknown.

A bit discouraging really.

Fortunately Ruth gave a good introduction to it in the tutorial. She said that most scholars believe that the *Didache* originated sometime before AD 100, probably in Syria. However, instead of being written by one author, it could have been compiled from other early works by a second-century scribe, possibly in Alexandria. At least one thing seems pretty certain though. It was intended to be a church manual, with moral advice, liturgical instructions, and disciplinary regulations.

Ignatius was the bishop of Antioch in Syria. Some time during the reign of the Emperor Trajan (AD 98-117) he was arrested and taken captive to Rome. While on the journey he wrote letters to a number of Christian communities; seven have survived.

Ruth said that the *Didache* seems to reflect an infant church. Travelling apostles, teachers, and prophets were still important, but a local church structure was gradually evolving. The Didachist (for want of something better to call him) wrote

> You must, then, elect for yourselves bishops and deacons who are a credit to the Lord, men who are gentle, generous, faithful and well tried. For their ministry to you is identical with that of the prophets and teachers. You must not, therefore, despise them, for along with the prophets and teachers they enjoy a place of honour among you . . .

'Well, my minister was only saying the other day that he gets a bit hurt when people in our church make a fuss about visiting evangelists but never seem to notice the work he does all year round', interrupted Maureen. 'Fancy it being just the same back then!'

Ruth smiled and went on to talk about the letters of Ignatius. In contrast to the *Didache,* they clearly show that a three-tiered hierarchy of bishop, presbyters or elders, and deacons had emerged in the church in Antioch.

> I exhort you: be eager to do everything in God's harmony, with the bishop presiding in the place of God and the presbytery in the place of the council of the apostles and the deacons, most sweet to me, entrusted with the service of Jesus Christ . . . (Letter to the Magnesians, 6)

All of you are to follow the bishop as Jesus Christ follows the Father, and the presbytery as the apostles. Respect the deacons as the command of God . . . (Letter to the Smyraeans, 8)

Ruth paused for breath and Frank butted in.

'Catholics wouldn't agree with what you just said about the Church hierarchy only coming about gradually. They reckon that Jesus made Peter the first pope and he went to Rome and started the Roman Catholic Church and everyone else has to obey it. A satanic conspiracy to undermine true Christianity, if you ask me.'

'Actually, I am a member of the Catholic Church,' responded Ruth calmly, 'and most of the books I read were written by Catholic historians. A lot of research has been done into the first centuries of the Church recently. I doubt whether any historian today would claim that Peter definitely founded the church in Rome, or that there definitely was a single bishop there in the first century. According to a letter from the church in Rome to the church in Corinth at the end of the century (1 Clement), it seems more likely that both churches had a two-tier hierarchy: bishops/elders and deacons. Likewise, Ignatius wrote to the Christian community in Rome without mentioning a single bishop, as he did in his other letters, so the monepiscopacy probably didn't emerge there until the mid-second century.'

Ruth looked thoughtful for a moment.

'However, I still believe that St Peter could have played a very significant role in the Roman church as an *apostle* rather than a bishop, and the church does seem to have felt that it inherited from St Peter and St Paul the pastoral care of other churches. Hence, the letter to the Corinthians is quite authoritative in tone, and Ignatius refers to the

9

Romans teaching others and ranking first in love and discipleship.'

'The fact that Rome was the capital of the empire must have been significant too', maintained Wade firmly. 'The Roman Christians certainly seemed to embrace the state's concern for law and order.'

Frank muttered something about not needing law and order if you are filled with the Holy Spirit, and Derek hurriedly asked if there was anything in particular that had struck us when we were reading the *Didache* and the letters of Ignatius.

'I was absolutely fascinated by the flexibility apparent in the *Didache*', replied Christobel immediately. 'It tells you all the Sermon-on-the-Mount-type things that you should do to become perfect, but then says: "Oh, well, if you can't do everything, do what you can". And about baptism it says: "Baptize in running water but if you do not have running water use some other. If you cannot in cold, then in warm. If you have neither, just pour water on the head three times in the name of the Father, Son and Holy Spirit." Isn't that thrillingly ecumenical?'

'And the eucharist seemed to be a proper, happy thanksgiving meal, with none of that depressing body-and-blood-of-Jesus talk, and only a sip of grape juice and a breadcrumb to eat', added Maureen.

'The Bible clearly implies that the only valid form of baptism is by complete immersion', said Frank in a disapproving tone. 'And we should never forget that it symbolizes our death with Christ, so that, Romans 6:4: "just as Christ was raised from the dead, we too may live a new life". And the communion service helps us remember the glorious BLOOD that covers our sins and saves us from eternal damnation. We should *never* forget the BLOOD.'

'I was struck', remarked Wade coldly, 'by the fact that the Didachist had to warn people not to be taken in by false prophets: "Not everybody who makes ecstatic utterances is a prophet, but only if he behaves like the Lord." If Christians spent more time imitating Jesus' care for the poor and the marginalized, and less time on spiritual ego trips, the Church and the world as a whole would be a lot better off.'

'Er . . . yes,' said Derek doubtfully, 'I take your point. What did you . . . er . . . think of Ignatius?'

Maureen snorted contemptuously.

'All that rubbish about "nothing being done without the bishop's permission" and "the bishop having to be obeyed as if he were God" made me want to throw up. Ignatius must have been a real arrogant so-and-so, just like my ex-husband!'

'He did come across as frightfully intolerant', agreed Christobel. 'He wouldn't have anything to do with the Christians who still wanted to adhere to Jewish customs, and he was terribly anti the poor Docetists, who believed that Christ did not have a real human body when on earth, but only the appearance of one.'

'And, unfortunately, history is usually written through the victors' eyes', put in Wade critically. 'The attacks in his letters were obviously propaganda against his opponents and it suited the mainstream Church to preserve them and suppress divergent views. However, what concerns me most about Ignatius is the fact that he was clearly promoting a very authoritarian episcopacy, far removed from the democratic origins of the Church, and he could have been very influential in the establishment of that kind of system in Rome and elsewhere, to the great detriment of Christianity.'

For once, Frank and Wade found themselves in agreement.

'Can you, though . . . er . . . see what perhaps could have

. . . er. . . motivated him?' asked Derek, looking troubled.

'I bet his mother spoilt him rotten and he couldn't bear not getting his own way', said Maureen at once. 'Just like my ex-husband.'

'He must have been mad', stated Christobel in a very definite tone. 'What sane person would actually *want* to be martyred as he claimed he did. Listen to this: "Let me be fodder for wild beasts . . . What a thrill I shall have from the wild beasts that are ready for me"! How more masochistic can you get? The poor man was probably abused as a child.'

Derek ran his fingers through his hair.

'I got the impression from Ignatius's letters that his main concern was to foster unity in the Church', said Ruth. 'Life must have been very difficult for Christians at the end of the first century. The apostles had died. Our Lord's second coming hadn't come. The Church was experiencing some persecution, and there were no copies of the New Testament to guide people. False prophets (like those mentioned in the *Didache*) were apparently leading some people astray. Ignatius tried to solve this problem by encouraging people to obey their bishop. Hopefully the bishop was a true Christian who could in turn teach the true faith to his followers.'

'Yes! Yes!' exclaimed Derek. 'And I think that in fairness to Ignatius his . . . er . . . exhortations to congregations to obey their bishops should not be considered in isolation from his conception of how a bishop should . . . er . . . behave. Did anyone find anything about that?

Silence.

Finally Ruth picked up her notes again.

'In his letter to Polycarp, bishop of Smyrna, Ignatius wrote among other things:

Make yourself the support of all and sundry, as the Lord is to you, and continue to bear lovingly with them all . . . Spend your time in constant prayer . . . See that nothing is ever done without consulting you, and do nothing yourself without consulting God . . . Address yourself to people personally, as is the way of God himself, and carry the infirmities of them all on your shoulders . . . Hold services more frequently, and hunt up everyone by name . . .'

'How big was his diocese then?' asked Maureen. 'My minister keeps calling me Irene. If he can't remember the names of the people in his one small church he'd be hopeless as a bishop.'

'The first bishops do seem to have been more like local church priests or pastors than administrators of great dioceses, Maureen', replied Ruth gently.

Derek nodded earnestly.

'Neville, Michael and Kirsty, you . . . er . . . haven't had a chance to say much. What did you think of Ignatius?'

'I'm afraid that I don't know much about bishops and episcopacy and things like that', said Kirsty, blushing, 'but I kind of liked Ignatius. I mean, the *Didache* seemed pretty dry and, well, like a textbook, but Ignatius's letters seemed like real letters written by a real person. He was so passionate in his beliefs and so brave about his approaching martyrdom. I wish that I had that kind of faith.'

I thought that Kirsty needed support, so before Wade could say something cutting I plucked up courage and said that I would like it too. Frank looked pleased, Maureen incredulous, Christobel concerned, Wade contemptuous, Neville embarrassed, and Derek and Ruth sympathetic.

'Well, on that . . . er . . . note I think that we had better finish up for today', Derek said.

Neville let out a sigh of relief.

On the way out Kirsty stopped me and said how grateful she was that I had backed her up.

'I felt way out of my depth at times—about six feet under. Do you think that it will get a bit easier as we go along?' she asked anxiously.

'Bound to', I said as confidently as possible.

She looked reassured.

Sure hope I'm right.

# WEEK·THREE

## What did the pagans think?

Today we were supposed to discuss the possible basis of pagan hostility to early Christians.

No one presented a tutorial paper, so it was just a general group discussion. I was really determined to say something this week, so as soon as Derek said 'What do you think?' I rushed in with a really good quote I found last night (in Everett Ferguson's *Backgrounds of Early Christianity*, p 475). I had expected to find that pagans thought the same way about Christians that a lot of people do today: a mob of boring, self-righteous do-gooders, who go to church on Sunday mornings when all normal people are sleeping in or mowing their lawn. Minucius Felix, however, accused Christians of indulging in gross immorality and cannibalism!

> An infant covered over with meal, that it may deceive the unwary, is placed before him who is to be stained with their rites; this infant is slain by the young pupil who has been urged on as if to harmless blows on the surface of the meal, with dark and secret wounds. Thirstily—O horror!—they lick up its blood; eagerly they divide its limbs . . . On a solemn day they assemble at the feast, with all their children, sisters, mothers, people of every sex and of every age. Then, after much feasting, when the fellowship has grown warm and the fervor of incestuous lust has grown hot with drunkenness, a

dog that has been tied to the chandelier is provoked, by throwing a small piece of offal beyond the length of a line by which he is bound, to rush and spring; and thus, the conscious light being overturned and extinguished in the shameless darkness, the connections of abominable lust . . .

As I was reading this to the group I had a sudden vision of my great-aunt Maud, pillar of the Methodist church for seventy years, taking part in a drunken orgy.

Very embarrassing. Tried to suppress laughter but ended up choking. The rest of the group looked on curiously, so I blurted out the unworthy thoughts about Aunt Maud. Fortunately everyone laughed, including Ruth.

*(I found out yesterday that she is a NUN!!!)*

As usual, Derek got us back on track.

'That is a good quotation from Minucius Felix, Michael. You all . . . er . . . know that he was a Christian who lived in the late second, early third centuries? He wrote a dialogue between a pagan and a Christian, and the passage that Michael just read is part, of course, of the pagan's attack on Christianity.'

And there was I thinking that poor old Min must have been one of the nastiest pagans who ever lived.

'It's rather ironic,' continued Derek, 'that most of the worst attacks on early Christians have survived because they were quoted by Christian writers in their defences of Christianity.'

'Just like when Christian groups carry on about films and things', interjected Maureen forcefully. 'All they end up doing is creating a big stir which gets more publicity for whatever it is they don't like.'

'Er . . . yes', agreed Derek hesitantly. 'But to return to Michael's very helpful quotation, what do you all . . . er . . .

think about the allegations it contained?'

'It's frightfully obvious that non-Christians misconstrued Christian terminology', asserted Christobel. 'They must have heard Christians talking about consuming the "body" and "blood" of Jesus during the eucharist and thought that some form of cannibalism was being practised. And all that absolutely wonderful talk in the New Testament about Christians loving one another, being the bride of Christ, greeting one another with holy kisses, and so on, could have been interpreted in an erotic sort of way.'

'It's amazing how easy it is for rumours to spread', said Ruth reflectively. (*I've never met a nun before.*)

'It sure is', affirmed Maureen with a vigorous nod. 'Only last year my best friend Enid had to go to hospital to have a gallstone out. She didn't want a lot of fuss made, so she just told me and our minister. However, he went and put her name on the prayer-chain list, in a vague sort of way. By the time it was my turn to pray, I discovered that we had been asking God to help Enid recover from her hysterectomy and nervous breakdown. She was real pleased when I told her that! Wouldn't go back to church for six weeks!'

'But if your friend had been completely open about her condition, the rumours probably wouldn't have started', observed Christobel. 'I think that it's awfully interesting that one of the main charges levelled against early Christians was that of secrecy. Minucius Felix made his pagan declare: "They are a secret tribe that lurks in darkness and shuns the light, silent in public, chattering in corners." Isn't that absolutely fascinating?'

'But if Christian groups were so secretive, how did they win converts?' asked Maureen in a disbelieving tone.

'Perhaps they didn't actually *intend* to form secret associations,' suggested Ruth, 'but it just looked as though they did. I read that they met quite a lot at night. I don't know exactly why. Perhaps they had businesses to attend to during the day, or they particularly wanted to pray together and celebrate the eucharist at dawn. In any case, they certainly didn't worship in public or have altars and temples like other religions, and their baptism and eucharist ceremonies were restricted to members. That could have seemed secretive to outsiders.'

(*She doesn't* look *like a nun. Aren't they supposed to wear things on their heads?*)

'And it was such a horribly sexist society', added Christobel, 'that Christian women might have concealed their faith from their husbands for fear of getting beaten up or stopped from going to Christian meetings.'

'And because Christianity wasn't a legal religion, Christians might have been afraid of being persecuted if they came out into the open too often', ventured Kirsty shyly.

Matthew 10:34 "I did not come to bring peace but a sword. I have come to turn a man against his father, a daughter against her mother, a daughter-in-law against her mother-in-law – a man's enemies will be members of his own household"', said Frank suddenly.

'The Romans greatly mistrusted groups that met at night', declared Wade with a disdainful glance at Frank. 'Night meetings were associated with seditious conspiracies, immorality, the practice of magic, and that kind of thing. Christian writers flatly denied that Christians were involved in any such thing, but I wonder whether there might have been some grounds for the pagans' suspicions. Take the allegations about Christians performing magic, for instance. Wacky supernatural things like talking in tongues, prophesying, and exorcising demons could have looked like magic to others.'

Christobel absolutely agreed.

'And as far as immorality is concerned,' went on Wade, 'even Christian writers admitted that some of the extreme Christian sects got involved in some very "off" activities. Just listen to this quotation from Epiphanius. It dates from the fourth century and describes a Gnostic-Christian sect.

> First they have their women in common . . . They serve rich food, meat and wine even if they are poor. When they thus ate together and so to speak filled up their veins to an excess they turn to passion. The man leaving his wife says to his own wife: Stand up and make love with the brother . . . Then the unfortunates unite with each other, and . . . after they have had intercourse in the passion of fornication they raise their own blasphemy toward heaven. The woman and the man take the fluid of the emission of the man . . .'

There was a lot more that was even more disgusting, about them using semen and aborted foetuses in their communion services. I don't think that Wade should have read it out in front of a nun.

'The devil doesn't want anyone to be saved so he tries to counterfeit and pervert Christian practices', said Frank in a sombre voice. 'Ephesians 6:12: "For our struggle is not against flesh and blood, but against the rulers, against the authorities, against the powers of this dark world and against the spiritual forces of evil in the heavenly realms . . ."'

Wade clenched his fists.

'We have looked at what you might call popular prejudice against Christians,' began Derek hurriedly, 'and, as Wade has helpfully pointed out, there may have been some basis for anti-Christian polemic. Er . . . no smoke without fire, so to speak. But what about the attacks on Christianity made by . . . er . . . educated people in society?'

'The satirist Lucian thought that Christians were frightfully gullible', responded Christobel. 'He wrote:

> The poor wretches have convinced themselves, first and foremost, that they are going to be immortal and live for all time, in consequence of which they despise death and even willingly give themselves into custody . . . Therefore they despise all things indiscriminately and consider them common property, receiving such doctrines traditionally without any definite evidence. So if any charlatan and trickster, able to profit by occasions, comes among them, he quickly acquires sudden wealth by imposing upon simple folk . . .'

'As we saw last week, there probably were false teachers and prophets around . . .', remarked Ruth slowly.

'I read about the philosopher Celsus who wrote in the late second century', interrupted Wade (*rather rudely, I thought; after all, she is a nun*). 'He really showed up some of the weaknesses inherent in Christianity. He argued that the Old Testament is full of stupid, illogical, and sometimes even offensive fables. God is supposed to be omnipotent, and yet he is portrayed as having human weaknesses; for example, he had to rest on the seventh day after creating the world! Turning to the New Testament, Celsus asked why, if God is omniscient and omnipresent, did he have to come to earth in the form of Jesus. To find out what was going on among human beings? And how can Christians say that they only worship one God when they worship Jesus as God's son too? Moreover, if Jesus really was God's son, why didn't God help him when he was on the cross? And if he really did rise from the dead, why didn't he appear to his critics instead of just to a (quote) "hysterical female and perhaps one other person too"?'

'What is the difference between Celsus and modern Christian theologians?' asked Christobel with a quick smile.

Wade thought seriously for a moment.

'Well, he didn't reject Jesus' miracles. He just thought that he must have picked up some sorcery tricks when he lived in Egypt, where that kind of thing was thought to be widespread.'

'1 Corinthians 1:25: "The foolishness of God is wiser than man's wisdom . . ."' began Frank ominously.

'What really interested me, however,' swept on Wade, 'was the fact that Celsus accused Christians of embracing the marginalized in society. He pointed out that other religions only wanted converts who were wise and pure of heart, but the Christians encouraged people who were stupid, uneducated and sinful to join their gatherings—which, in his eyes, included women, slaves and little children!'

'The Christians knew that "all have sinned and fall short of the glory of God", but God sent his Son to earth to die for their sins so that they might be saved', said Frank joyfully. 'They would have been going around telling the pagans that they were going to hell and the only way that they could be saved was by accepting Jesus into their hearts . . .'

'You certainly would have been saying that, if you'd been around then', interrupted Maureen.

General laughter. Frank looked pleased.

'But Satan doesn't want people to be saved, so he would have stirred up opposition. The pagans wouldn't have liked hearing about hell, and they would have hated the Christians who were rejoicing in being saved . . .'

'Can you blame them?' hissed Neville to me.

'Sorry, Neville, what was that?' asked Derek innocently.

Neville turned bright red and muttered something about Christianity appearing exclusive.

Wade seized on the word 'exclusive'.

'That really got up the Romans' noses, the fact that Christians were claiming that there was only one god, when for generations their ancestors had been worshipping dozens. The Jews were also monotheistic, of course, but, while the Romans despised them, they did at least respect the fact that Judaism was an ancient faith. The Christians, on the other hand, were raving on about a convicted criminal, who had been executed by the Roman authorities a few years before, being the son of the one true god! Minucius Felix's pagan said that "all must feel grieved and indignant and annoyed that certain people – people, too, ignorant of learning, unlettered, and unacquainted even with the meanest arts—should pronounce definitely upon the universe and the supreme power . . ."'

'Yes', agreed Christobel enthusiastically. 'I tried to imagine the other day what it would have been like being a Roman in the second century, and I came to the conclusion (as a pagan) that the Christians were arrogant, ignorant pains in the bum!'

'Er . . . thank you, Wade and Christobel, for that contribution', said Derek in a faint voice. 'Unfortunately we are running out of time. Has anyone got anything else that they would like to say about hostility to Christianity?'

'It all boils down to the opposition of the devil!' stated Frank adamantly.

'Oh, I don't believe in the devil,' said Christobel blithely, 'at least, not as the personification of evil. What I think happened was that there was a tragic lack of understanding between pagans and Christians. People get so terribly rigid in their views and won't see that there are elements of truth in all religious faiths. I try to be totally open and unbiased myself, and I wish that more Christians today would do the same.'

Wade nodded.

'But, in the final analysis, the basis of hostility to early Christianity was the fact that Christians were aiding and upholding the marginalized, and hence they were seen as subversive to the prevailing social order. I only wish that the same could be said of most Christians in the twentieth century.'

'I'm just glad that I'm alive now and not then', said Kirsty in a heartfelt way. 'The teasing I get for going to youth group doesn't seem nearly as bad now as I once thought it was.'

Frank and I happened to be the last to leave. He said in a significant voice that it was a pity that we had a non-Christian in our midst. I asked who, and he looked at me with surprise.

'Wade, of course!'

'Oh,' said I, 'I think he's a candidate for ordination in the Uniting Church. He belongs to the trendy wing that puts a lot of emphasis on social action.'

'It's no good helping people's material needs if their souls are going to hell', replied Frank with a grave shake of his head. 'There are a lot of non-Christians in the Uniting Church.' ???

# WEEK·FOUR

## The government's reaction

Poor Kirsty had to lead today's discussion on government
policy towards Christians, the motives behind the
persecutions and their consequences. She seemed very
nervous but did a good job.

She began by looking at the first century. Confessed that
she couldn't find much evidence of persecution then, just
Nero and the fire that swept through Rome in AD 64.
According to someone called Tacitus, it was rumoured that
Nero himself had started the fire. In response, he tried to
shift the blame onto the Christians, who, as we saw last
week, were already unpopular with many people.

'And hence, Christians were the victims more of prejudice
and misunderstanding than of government policy',
concluded Christobel triumphantly. 'But it backfired on
Nero, because Tacitus says that he tortured them so terribly
that "even for criminals who deserved extreme and
exemplary punishment, there arose a feeling of compassion;
for it was not, as it seemed, for the public good, but to glut
one man's cruelty, that they were being destroyed".'

'Yes', said Maureen. 'He held a garden party one night and
drove guests around his garden in his chariot. The lighting
was provided by burning Christians.'

Kirsty shuddered.

'What is really significant about the Tacitus story, however, is the fact that Christians were clearly being distinguished from the Jews', interjected Wade firmly. 'The Jewish religion was tolerated by the Romans, and as Christianity was initially seen as an internal Jewish sect, it shared Jewish legal protection. Tacitus's account of the fire in Rome is the earliest indication we have that the situation had changed.'

Derek nodded, and confirmed that this was indeed the first recorded official persecution of Christianity, and that it has been traditionally thought that Peter and Paul were among the Christians put to death at the time. But the persecution may not have lasted long (Nero died in AD 68), and it may not have spread beyond Rome.

Kirsty then tentatively mentioned the Emperor Domitian, who ruled from AD 81 to 96. It is not known for sure whether the people he persecuted were Christians or Jews, but he insisted on being called 'lord and god', which must have made things very difficult for Christians.

'Arrogant pig', muttered Maureen.

'He probably didn't believe that he actually was a god', asserted Wade. 'Claiming to be divine was just a wonderful way of consolidating his position in a state destablilized by civil war. But, in any case, I don't think that he was particularly concerned about Christianity. There is a story that he interrogated some relatives of Jesus, and when he found that they were only poor peasants who believed in a kingdom not of this world, he despised them so much that he didn't think them worth persecuting.'

'Matthew 19:30: "Many who are first will be last, and many who are last will be first"', quoted Frank fervently.

That seemed to be enough on Domitian. Kirsty then divulged that Pliny, a governor of a Roman province, once wrote a letter to Emperor Trajan (AD 98-117) asking for his guidance because he didn't know what to do with Christians. Had any of us read the letter, and what did we think?

Ruth remarked that it was interesting that Pliny could not find the Christians guilty of anything other than obstinacy, although on those grounds alone he had put some to death.

'The Romans placed great emphasis on obedience to the state', declared Wade. 'Refusing to obey the governor would have been a very serious crime. However, what I particularly noted in Pliny's letter was his concern that Christianity had spread through the country to such an extent that the temples were deserted and the livelihood of those associated with non-Christian worship was threatened. Clearly, therefore, political and economic factors lay behind government opposition to Christians.'

'Inspired by the devil', added Frank.

'How did Trajan . . . er . . . reply to Pliny?' asked Derek quickly.

Christobel said that he must have been awfully nice, because he told Pliny not to seek out Christians and not to listen to anonymous accusations against them. Furthermore, if they *were* arrested, they were to be given an opportunity to recant and pay their respects to the Roman gods.

'But if you were arrested and refused to renounce Christ you could still be killed', said Maureen hotly. 'I don't call that "awfully nice". If there is one thing I can't stand it's governments who try to control the way people think. I find it hard enough to be civil to the woman from the Bureau of Statistics who keeps coming to nosey out my personal affairs, but if anyone tries to tell me what to think I tell them to naff off.'

Christobel agreed that freedom of thought was an absolutely vital, inalienable right of personkind.

'Living in a Western democracy we take for granted freedom to worship God', remarked Frank solemnly. 'But there are still many places in the world where Christians are persecuted. In Asia . . .'

'Yes, that's well worth . . . er . . . remembering, Frank', intervened Derek. 'Now, Trajan's policy was reaffirmed by his successor Hadrian and seems to have continued until the mid-third century. The main point I want you to . . . er . . . note is that Christians do not seem to have suffered continuous, systematic persecution. Outbreaks of persecution undoubtedly did occur, but they seem to have been rather . . . er . . . spasmodic and local in character.'

'And motivated by misunderstandings and popular prejudice', continued Christobel with a breezy smile. 'As Tertullian commented in the late second or early third century: "If the Tiber rises too high or the Nile too low, the cry is 'The Christians to the lion'. All of them to a single lion?"'

I think that was meant to be a second-century joke. Only Neville sniggered.

Moving on to the third century, Kirsty said that Decius became emperor in 249 and started a more systematic persecution of Christians in the following year. Christian leaders were imprisoned and everyone in the empire was required to obtain a certificate (a *libellus*) showing that they had made a formal sacrifice to the Roman gods.

'Another arrogant pig', observed Maureen caustically. 'Power must have gone to his head.'

'Inspired by the devil', added Frank.

'That's only a faith statement', replied Wade, grinding his teeth. 'It is obvious to anyone who has *properly* studied Roman history that the mid-third century was a very difficult time in the empire, politically, socially and economically.

There was constant warfare against the Germanic tribes in the north and the Persians in the east, and oppressively high taxation was required to maintain the army. There was also a series of natural disasters like plagues and famines, and the political situation was highly unstable. At one stage there were twenty different emperors in forty years! Decius came to power in what was virtually a military *coup d'état*. Seeing that it was a time of great crisis, he tried to stabilize the situation and restore Roman greatness. Naturally enough, that included making sure that the Roman gods had their traditional place of honour in society and that all the inhabitants of the empire were loyal, devout citizens.'

'And the number of Christians had grown to such an extent that they now posed a real challenge to fundamentalist pagans in the empire', enthused Christobel.

Derek agreed, and Kirsty asked what we thought the effects of the Decian persecution were.

'The Christians would have been enormously strengthened by the ordeal', declared Frank excitedly. 'I heard a missionary from China say the other day that the church there is like bamboo – the more the authorities cut it down, the more it grows. It would have been exactly the same in the third century, only I don't know whether they had any bamboo in Rome.'

'Actually,' remarked Wade coldly, 'the Church almost totally collapsed. The leaders who weren't killed went into hiding, and most of their flock managed to obtain their *libelli*, through bribery or downright submission. Overall, very few lives appear to have been lost.'

Christobel absolutely agreed, but noted that Frend said in his book *The Rise of Christianity* (p 328), that the years 248 to 260 were a real watershed in the history of the Church. To prove her point she quoted:

In retrospect, the Decian persecution emerges as the real testing point between the Church and the empire. Had the Church collapsed, it could scarcely have recovered. As it was, the combination of military and economic disasters took a heavier toll on traditional pagan society than they did on the Church. The latter proved triumphantly resilient. Its worldwide organization, its economic power, and its martyr-tradition were proof against persecution and mass temporary apostasies. By 256 it had become stronger than it had been before persecution broke out. The 'unlawful association' (*religio illicita*) was now a rival to the empire itself. By the time Diocletian threw down the final challenge in 303, the battle had been lost.

'That's just what I said', argued Frank. 'The Church came through stronger.'

'Decius, of course, died in battle against the Goths in 251 . . .' began Ruth.

Frank exuberantly shouted HOORAY! and PRAISE THE LORD!

'And his successors did not immediately persecute Christians,' continued Ruth calmly, 'until Valerian began arresting Christian leaders and confiscating church property in 257.'

'And, funnily enough, he also had a fairly horrid death,' observed Kirsty, 'captured by the Persians in 260, I think. His son stopped persecuting Christians altogether and even let them have their property back.'

'It was obviously more important to unite the citizens of the empire against the Goths and the Persians than to pursue minor religious issues', said Wade quickly, breaking in before Frank could give another hooray. 'And that continued to be the case until Diocletian came to power in 284. A great soldier and conservative reformer, he tried, like Decius, to turn the clock back to the days of Rome's greatness. Eventually he was encouraged by his assistant Galerius to wipe out Christianity. In 303 Christians were forbidden to meet and ordered to surrender their Bibles and liturgical books, and churches were destroyed. In 304 everyone in the empire was required to sacrifice to the traditional gods on pain of death. Persecutions continued until Galerius was forced to sign an edict of toleration on his deathbed in 311' (Frank did manage to get in a 'Praise the Lord' this time), 'and Constantine and Licinius signed the Edict of Milan in 313.'

'What effects did the persecutions have on Christianity?' asked Kirsty again.

'They must have been terrible for many people,' replied Ruth, 'but I got the impression that they weren't effectively carried out throughout the empire. The East seemed to suffer much more than the West.'

'They would have really united the Christians', said Frank confidently. 'Brought them together against a common enemy . . .'

'Er . . . I am sorry to say that that did not quite . . . er . . . happen, Frank, in the mid-third century or the early fourth', answered Derek.

'Absolutely not', agreed Christobel. 'When the persecutions finished, some horrid self-righteous Christians, who hadn't given in to the authorities, refused to let those who had weakened come back into the Church.'

'Ah', said Frank, thinking this over. 'You are forgetting that Jesus said: "Whoever disowns me before men, I will disown him before my Father in heaven" (Matthew 10:32). A person is saved by the simple act of confessing with his mouth and believing in his heart that Jesus is Lord (Romans 10:9). To deny Jesus is to side with the devil.'

'So you could sit back and watch your wife and children being tortured and killed even though you knew that you could set them free by making a meaningless gesture to a non-existent pagan deity?' asked Maureen incredulously.

'I trust that I would not be found wanting', replied Frank solemnly.

'I'm glad I'm not your wife!' exclaimed Christobel. 'I would certainly have found you wanting. But, in my opinion, what was even worse than not letting repentant Christians back into the Church after the persecutions, was the fairly widespread belief that you could not retain your salvation if you sinned after baptism.'

'Who could possibly be saved then?' demanded Maureen.

'People postponed their baptism until their deathbeds', said Wade in contemptuous tones.

'What if they were run over by a chariot and couldn't get to a priest in time?' pursued Maureen, visibly stunned.

'Alas, they went to hell', mocked Wade.

'Well', said Maureen, outraged. 'So much for the prodigal son and all that love and forgiveness nonsense in the New Testament!'

'The prodigal son hadn't been baptized and he hadn't denied his father', pointed out Frank. 'Just wasted his money.'

'Well, if anyone tries to tell me that God doesn't love and forgive me, I'll give them a piece of my mind', declared Maureen heatedly.

'This was a serious issue for early Christians to grapple with', said Ruth pensively. 'Should the Church be a society of saints or a school for sinners? Fortunately (as I know I'm far from being a saint) Rome eventually affirmed the latter view.'

'And started up penances and things, which are totally unscriptural', added Frank belligerently.

'Unfortunately we have run out of time', said Derek, looking rather desperately at his watch. 'Is there anything else that you would like to say, Kirsty?'

'I just sort of wondered what you all would have done if you'd lived during the persecutions', responded Kirsty bashfully.

'As I said before, I hope that I would not have been found wanting', said Frank adamantly.

'If you want my opinion,' stated Christobel, looking at Frank with a mixture of pity and revulsion, 'this whole issue is a storm in a teacup. It's what goes on in your heart that God really cares about. I am absolutely convinced that I could have thrown my pinch of incense onto the pagan altar without it having the slightest effect on my true spiritual life.'

Wade agreed, and maintained that it was far more important to concentrate on helping the marginalized than provoking the authorities by making meaningless heroic gestures.

'If you ask me,' remarked Maureen astringently, 'I must admit that if anyone ordered me to sacrifice I would probably lose my temper and tell them to get stuffed, and to hell with the consequences!'

'Er . . . that is very brave of you, Maureen', commented Derek. 'And, er . . . Neville, what would you have done?'

'You wouldn't have seen me for dust', said Neville simply.

Derek looked at me, and I said something about keeping Neville company. We could have run to the hills.

'On second thoughts,' interjected Maureen, 'hire a chariot and I'll come too. Can't run because of my corns.'

When pressed, Ruth said that, like Wade, she probably would have tried not to provoke the authorities, but, if she had been arrested, she hoped that she would have had enough courage not to deny her Lord.

Derek admitted that he felt the same way.

That only left Kirsty, who turned bright red.

'Would you mind if I came with you and Neville and Maureen?' she asked me.

'Glad to have you on board', said I.

'Better hire a big chariot then, dear', Maureen advised Neville. 'I'll bring the food. And will you let us back into the Church when the persecutions finish?' she suddenly turned on Frank.

'Oh, he'll be dead by then', said Christobel cheerfully.

'No such luck', murmured Wade.

Frank didn't appear to hear him but thought carefully for a moment.

'Maureen, Neville, Michael and Kirsty *might* be able to rejoin the fellowship because they didn't actually deny Jesus with their mouths, although I'm afraid that running away might amount to the same thing. However, Chrisobel and Wade's case is much more serious.'

Christobel gathered up her books and wafted to the door. 'Remember, the first might be last and the last first', she said mysteriously to Frank as she floated out. ???

Went to have a cup of coffee with Wade and Neville. Wade went on and on about Frank, and what pains Pentecostals are. Felt guilty afterwards that I hadn't said anything to defend Frank and the charismatic movement, which I am really quite interested in. But, honestly, Jesus does have compassion on sinners, even those who deny him under pressure and then repent afterwards. Doesn't he???

# Week·Five

## The ultimate witness

Tutorial topic today: How was martyrdom regarded in the early Church? It was Maureen's turn to start the discussion, which she did in her usual down-to-earth fashion. Just asked the question: Who is your favourite martyr, and why?

Christobel immediately said Blandina, because she was a woman. In fact, Christobel went on to point out, not only was Blandina a woman, but she was a poor, seemingly insignificant slave girl, which really goes to show that the greatest Christians in the early Church were not all the bigoted old bishops given the name Church Fathers.

Maureen suggested that Christobel read the story of Blandina's sufferings and death from the account of the martyrs of Lyons and Vienne in A *New Eusebius*, which she did, really eloquently.

> But the entire fury of the crowd, governor and soldiers fell upon Sanctus . . . and upon Maturus . . . and upon Blandina through whom Christ showed that things which appear mean and unsightly and despicable in the eyes of men are accounted worthy of great glory in the sight of God, through love towards him, a love which showed itself in power and did not boast itself in appearance. For when we were all afraid, and her mistress according to the flesh (who was herself a combatant in the ranks of the martyrs) was in a state of agony,

lest the weakness of her body should render her unable even to make a bold confession, Blandina was filled with such power that those who by turns kept torturing her in every way from dawn till evening were worn out and exhausted, and themselves confessed defeat from lack of aught else to do to her; they marvelled that the breath still remained in a body all mangled and covered with gaping wounds, and they testified that a single form of torture was sufficient to render life extinct, let alone such and so many. But the blessed woman, like a noble champion, in confession regained her strength; and for her, to say 'I am a Christian, and with us no evil finds a place' was refreshment and rest and insensibility to her lot.

'Wasn't she incredibly brave?' remarked Christobel in thrilling accents. 'And there's more. That poor women was taken to the amphitheatre and

suspended on a stake, was exposed as food to the wild beasts which were let loose against her. Even to look on her, as she hung cross-wise in earnest prayer, wrought great eagerness in those who were contending [against the beasts], for in their conflict they beheld with their outward eyes in the form of their sister him who was crucified for them, that he might persuade those who believe in him that all who suffer for the glory of Christ have unbroken fellowship with the living God. And as none of the wild beasts then touched her, she was taken down from the stake and cast again into prison, being kept for another conflict, that she might conquer in still further contests, and so both render irrevocable the sentence passed on the crooked serpent, and encourage the brethren – she the small, the weak, the despised, who had put on Christ the great and invincible Champion, and who in many rounds vanquished the adversary and through conflict was crowned with the crown of incorruptibility.

'The writer then describes other amazingly wonderful martyrs but gets back to Blandina:

After all these, finally on the last day of the single combats Blandina was again brought in, in the company of Ponticus, a lad about fifteen years old. They had also been fetched in every day to view the tortures of the others. The heathen tried to force them to swear by their idols, and as they remained firm and set them at naught, the multitude was so infuriated at them that it had neither compassion for the youth of the boy nor respect for the sex of the woman. Nay, they exposed them to every cruelty and brought them through the entire round of tortures, again and again trying to force them to swear. But this they were unable to accomplish; for Ponticus, encouraged by his sister (so that the heathen themselves saw that it was she who was urging him on and strengthening him), having nobly endured every kind of torture gave up his spirit. But the blessed Blandina last of all, having, like a high-born mother, exhorted her children and sent them forth victorious to the King, travelled herself along the same path of conflicts as they did, and hastened to them, rejoicing and exulting at her departure, like one bidden to a marriage supper, rather than cast to the wild beasts. And after the scourging, after the wild beasts, after the frying-pan, she was at last thrown into a basket and presented to a bull. For a time the animal tossed her, but she had now lost all perception of what was happening, thanks to the hope she cherished, her grasp of the objects of her faith, and her intercourse with Christ. Then she too was sacrificed, and even the heathen themselves acknowledged that never in their experience had a woman endured so many terrible sufferings.'

Maureen thanked Christobel for reading so well, and commented that Blandina was one of about forty-seven or forty-eight Christians who died in Lyons in Gaul in 177. She then asked Kirsty to name her favourite martyr. Thought Kirsty looked rather pale, but she said that she liked the story of Polycarp best. His death wasn't as gruesome as Blandina's, and he seemed like a really nice old man.

When asked to elaborate, Kirsty said that when Polycarp was arrested he refused to deny that Jesus was his Lord but declared: 'Eighty-six years have I served him, and he has done me no wrong: how then can I blaspheme my King who saved me?' Then the Holy Spirit helped him face his death. When he entered the stadium people heard a voice say quite clearly, 'Be strong, Polycarp, and play the man', and when he was burning on the stake and the executioner stabbed him with a dagger, a dove flew out of his body.

'It isn't known for sure whether the dove-bit formed part of the original text or not,' observed Wade discouragingly, 'and in any case it was probably just a way of describing the soul departing from the corpse. Likewise, the mysterious voice could have been made by anyone in the crowd. The real significance of the Polycarp story is that it reveals that martyrs were venerated in the second century. Members of Polycarp's church at Smyrna obviously thought that his death was so important that they wrote an account of it to send to other congregations; they claimed that his bones were "more valuable than precious stones and finer than gold"; and they planned to meet every year to celebrate the "birthday" of his martyrdom.'

'Catholics still do that', said Frank. 'And pray to martyrs as if they were God, and worship bits of their bones and clothes and things. My wife's aunt reckoned that she had a piece of some saint-or-another's pillowcase in a glass jar, and you would have thought that it was the holy of holies the way she went on about it. It was kept on the mantelpiece in her sitting-room and no one was ever allowed to go in there except the priest when he visited once a week.'

Ruth quietly pointed out that the Christians at Smyrna clearly stated that they did not hold martyrs in the same esteem as Jesus.

'The authorities were reluctant to give them Polycarp's body for fear that they would begin to worship him instead of Jesus, but they retorted that they could never forsake Christ, "For him, as Son of God, we adore; the martyrs, as disciples and imitators of the Lord, we reverence as they deserve on account of their unsurpassable loyalty to their own King and Teacher".'

'Yeah, well, that might have been so then, but I still reckon saint-worshipping got out of hand in the Catholic Church later', maintained Frank stubbornly. 'Especially as "saint" is just another word for Christian in the New Testament. Ephesians 1:3 . . .'

'Who is your favourite martyr?' asked Maureen abruptly.

A joyful smile spread across Frank's face.

'You can't go past Jesus, the Lamb of God who died so that we can be saved . . .'

'I . . . er . . . think that Maureen meant one of the early Christians, Frank, not our Lord', intervened Derek.

'Well, Stephen then', responded Frank amicably. 'Acts 7:55-60: "But Stephen, full of the Holy Spirit, looked up to heaven . . ."'

'Stephen is a very . . . er . . . inspiring example, but did you find a martyr that you particularly admired when you were reading the accounts of martyrdoms in the early Church, that is . . . er . . . one that is not in the New Testament?'

'Oh, I never read any other book than the Bible', said Frank blithely. 'Made that commitment six years ago when I was saved, and I've never felt the slightest bit tempted to break it.'

Suddenly remembered the novel that I'm half-way through reading, and felt condemned – all that passion, power and violence!

'I absolutely adore reading,' cried Christobel, 'and I can never get enough books – never! I've spent an absolute fortune on textbooks but I know that they're worth every single penny because they're absolutely fascinating and it's so frightfully necessary to broaden your mind . . .'

Felt guilty again. I usually just borrow books from the library. I can barely understand the theology ones, and after a chapter or two of history the lines often start blurring and I find myself dozing off. I've given up trying to read in bed or in my beanbag, but even at my desk it's pretty heavy going.

Stopped daydreaming about books to find that Derek, in a very worried voice, was trying to explain to Frank that he thought that it would be very difficult to study (and pass) tertiary subjects without reading any book but the Bible, even subjects run by the Theology Department.

'Bloody impossible!' muttered Wade. 'Especially in the Theology Department!'

'Oh, no,' said Frank unabashed, 'I pray about each tutorial topic and seek guidance from the Lord. John 16:13: "When he, the Spirit of truth comes, he will guide you into all truth." And the answers to today's tutorial topic, about Christian attitudes to martyrdom, were so obvious I didn't even have to pray about them! The Christians would have "rejoiced because they had been counted worthy of suffering disgrace for the Name" (Acts 5:41). They would have realized that they were being united with Christ in his death in order that they would be united with him in his resurrection

(Romans 6:5; 8:17). They would have understood that suffering was a natural part of discipleship and that it helped carry the good news to non-Christians (2 Corinthians 4 and 6). And they would have been comforted by 2 Thessalonians 1:6-9:

> God is just: he will pay back trouble to those who trouble you . . . This will happen when the Lord Jesus is revealed from heaven in blazing fire with his powerful angels. He will punish those who do not know God and do not obey the gospel of our Lord Jesus. They will be punished with everlasting destruction . . .

'However, more than that, it is promised in Revelation 20 that those who suffer martyrdom for Jesus' sake will actually sit on thrones in heaven and be given authority to judge non-Christians. Isn't that fantastic? Can you blame Christians for wanting to be martyred?'

'Of course, those ideas were not unique to Christianity', declared Wade, with barely suppressed frustration. 'Jewish apocalyptic literature from the first and second centuries BC reveals that many Jews were trying to justify their oppressed state by highlighting the redemptive value of suffering and the imminent destruction of their enemies in the great end-time battle. Christian writings were obviously influenced by that literature, especially Mark 13 and Revelation. And the account of the deaths of Eleazar and the seven young men and their mother in 4 Maccabees also greatly influenced Christian views on martyrdom. The description of Blandina, "like a high-born mother, exhorting her children and sending them victorious to the King", is almost a direct quote from 4 Maccabees.'

Christobel agreed, and strongly recommended that Frank

read 4 Maccabees as it was practically Old Testament anyway.

'But what I absolutely cannot accept, Frank, is that ALL Christians would have liked to have been martyred', she continued with an airy gesture. 'I would truly-ruly LOVE to be awfully brave like Blandina, but I have the most lowering suspicion that at the slightest HINT of torture I'd say ABSOLUTELY ANYTHING to get free. And it's no use saying that I would be comforted by the thought of God punishing my enemies, because I believe that God loves EVERYBODY and I try to love them too. And I've had to do jury duty twice and utterly hated it, so the thought of being stuck on a throne in heaven judging non-Christians doesn't turn me on either.'

'What I can't understand', began Kirsty with an embarrassed blush, 'is the way some early Christians talked about martyrdom as if it were a sort of baptism necessary for true discipleship. I mean, when Ignatius of Antioch was writing about being thrown to the lions he said things like, he wanted to "get to God", be "a real disciple of Jesus Christ", and not just be called a Christian but "actually *be* one" and he'd been a bishop for years and years. I was taught in Sunday School that Jesus died for our sins once and for all, and we sort of acknowledge that when we are baptized in water. Do we really need to be "baptized in blood" as well?'

'I suppose that idea goes back to that rubbish we talked about last week, Christians not being able to sin after baptism and all that', grumbled Maureen. 'They probably thought that baptism in blood gave them a second chance.'

'Jesus certainly died on the cross to save you, Kirsty,' intervened Frank earnestly, 'but he also said: "If anyone would come after me, he must deny himself and take up his cross and follow me. For whoever wants to save his life will

lose it, but whoever loses his life for me will find it"
(Matthew 16:24, 25).'

Maureen was struck by a sudden thought.

'And when the pagans stopped throwing Christians to the
lions, the Christians started going out into the desert and
becoming monks and nuns and missionaries and things like
that.'

'Well, I believe that we all have different gifts, and God
wants us to use them in different ways', said Christobel
firmly. 'I'm absolutely sure that I'd make a frightful nun or
missionary. Of course, I think that Mother Teresa and
people like her are absolutely marvellous, and I give
donations to support them and that kind of thing, but I
refuse to be made to feel guilty about also spending money
on clothes, jewellery and so on. The basic issue is really
getting your priorities right, and I spend an awful lot of time
on spiritual things.'

Thought Derek looked rather tired and drawn. He said
that once more we had almost run out of time, and would
Maureen like to say anything more about early Christian
attitudes to martyrdom.

Maureen replied that, like Christobel, she thought that all
early Christians probably hadn't thought alike. Some seem
to have been really keen to die for Christ, while others ran
away, or denied that they were Christians when they were
arrested. Overall, however, they did seem to think that
imitating Jesus was pretty important.

'But, personally, I'm not that impressed by fanatics like
Ignatius', she concluded reflectively. 'He keeps reminding
me of my ex-husband. I prefer the story of Polycarp because,
like Jesus, he didn't go out of his way to get arrested (in fact,
the writer of his martyrdom story rebukes people who do).
However, when he was betrayed by a member of his own

household (again, like Jesus, funnily enough), he didn't put up any resistance. He was really dignified in front of the authorities and really brave about being killed. And whatever the truth about the miracles that were said to have occurred when he died, it must have been great publicity for Christianity, all those pagans seeing a man prepared to die for his faith. Tertullian once said that "the blood of Christians is seed". That certainly seemed to be true in the early Church.'

On that sort of positive note we finished. On the way out I asked Neville what he would have done if he'd been a Christian back then who got arrested.

'Prayed that the lions were very hungry', he answered enigmatically. ???

# Week·Six

## Hellenistic culture

Really worked hard preparing for this tutorial. First had to find what 'Hellenistic' means. It seems to relate to the Greek culture spread by Alexander the Great when he was busy conquering the world in the fourth century BC. When the Romans in turn conquered the Greeks and almost everybody else in the first and second centuries BC, they were clearly awfully good at winning battles and building roads, bridges and aqueducts. However, their culture left a lot to be desired, at least as far as the Greeks were concerned. The Romans got an inferiority complex about this, and, rapt with Hellenism, tried to pretend that it belonged to them too. Not everyone was fooled. A guy named Horace (I couldn't find his surname) commented: 'Captured Greece took captive her savage conqueror and brought civilization to rustic Latium.'

What did the Jews think of this? Apparently it used to be thought that Hellenism and Judaism were dead opposites, but most scholars now agree that not even the Jews were immune to Greek culture. The problem is, to what degree did they accept it? Some Jews seem to have been determined to practise only Jewish customs and shun anything remotely Greek, while others couldn't see anything wrong with watching the odd Greek play or popping into the local sauna.

Christians also seem to have been divided over whether they should stick to traditional Jewish ways of doing things or be a bit more flexible. In *Antioch and Rome* Raymond Brown says that *at least* four different groups of Christians are apparent in the New Testament writings:

1. 'Jewish Christians and their Gentile converts, who insisted on full observance of the Mosaic Law, including circumcision.' In other words, the *ultraconservatives*. A Gentile had to become a Jew to become a Christian.
2. 'Jewish Christians and their Gentile converts, who did not insist on circumcision but did require converted Gentiles to keep some Jewish observances.' The *moderately conservatives*. James the brother of Jesus and Peter probably belonged to this group.
3. 'Jewish Christians and their Gentile converts, who did not insist on circumcision and did not require observance of the Jewish food laws.' The *moderates*. E.g. Paul.
4. 'Jewish Christians and their Gentile converts, who did not insist on circumcision or observance of the Jewish food laws and who saw no abiding significance in Jewish cult and feasts.' The *liberals*.

And I thought that denominations only became a problem for Christians when Henry VlII wanted a divorce!

One fairly important aspect of Hellenistic culture seems to have been philosophy. We were asked to look particularly at Platonism and Neoplatonism in our tutorial, so here goes.

**Platonism** was begun by Plato who was born about 428 BC. He was a disciple of Socrates (another famous philosopher) who set up his own school of philosophy in Athens, which became known as the Academy.

Tried to work out the gist of his thought. He seems to have had a thing about the world of our senses being imperfect and unreliable. To him, true reality lay in pure, unchanging ideas or forms (e.g. perfect beauty, perfect wisdom, perfect courage, etc.). Above all, he believed that there was one supreme, absolute idea or form: the Good. I suppose that was kind of like God.

Plato also thought that our souls are immortal. They pre-exist before our birth and they will survive death. The body is actually the prison of the soul, but a strong soul can (through a lot of contemplation) transcend the physical world toward the ideal and the eternal.

To describe this, Plato said that we are like people chained to the inside wall of a cave. All we can see are the shadows of reality on the wall (which we think are real), made by things passing by a fire at the entrance to the cave. A few people manage to break free and discover the wonderful world outside the cave, but others are scared by the light and want to stay in the darkness. When the ones who go outside return, ecstatic, to tell those inside about the beauty they have seen, they are mocked and sometimes even put to death.

In other words, philosophers who discover spiritual realities are given a hard time when they try to convince others that what they say is true.

**Neoplatonism** is associated with Plotinus, who lived in Egypt from about AD 205 to 270 and added quite a bit to Platonism from other philosophical schools.

Basically he seems to have wanted to place everything in a hierarchical structure. At the top of his hierarchy he put the great, transcendent One (like Plato's Good). Then, continuously emanating from the One is Thought or Mind. Emanating from Thought or Mind is Universal Soul. Emanating from Universal Soul are World Soul and our individual souls. Our souls have a deep, inner longing to return to the One. Through a lot of hard work (contemplation, suppressing desires, etc.) some can eventually get there.

Neville talked a lot about Platonism and Neoplatonism in his tutorial paper. He came into the room, sat straight down, and began to read it in a dead monotone voice. It was incredible – he didn't seem to pause for breath once in twenty minutes! Unfortunately I just got totally confused. There was something about apples not really being apples, but only a perfect idea of an apple really being an apple.

When Neville finally came to a halt, gasped for breath, and slapped his folder shut, Derek thanked him for all his work and said that apples made a very good analogy.

Maureen, however, frankly admitted that she hadn't understood a word he'd said.

'Don't think I'm criticizing you, dear,' she said kindly to Neville, 'it's probably just that I'm dumb, but all that apple talk reminded me of my ex-brother-in-law. He was always saying obscure things like that. I'm finding that one of the really good things about a divorce is that you no longer have to see all the in-laws you've never really liked.'

'Er . . . I'm sorry that you had difficulty grasping philosophical concepts, Maureen', said Derek. 'How did the rest of you go?'

'I found it absolutely fascinating', cooed Christobel. '"Philosophy" actually means "the love of wisdom", and I just love wisdom, so I must have a natural bent for philosophy.

What particularly struck me about those wonderful early philosophers was that they were Seeking After Truth, which is exactly what I am doing too. As Socrates said: "The unexamined life is not worth living."'

47

'He also said: "I am consumed by the fact of my own ignorance"', muttered Neville, but I don't think that Christobel heard him.

'Well, they didn't find the truth,' interjected Frank, 'because they didn't find Jesus. The early Christians weren't influenced by philosophy. They were influenced by the Holy Spirit.'

'That is only a faith statement!' said Wade through clenched teeth.

'I. . . er . . . respect Frank's right to believe that the early Christians were filled with the Holy Spirit', intervened Derek hastily, 'but, you know, Frank, Christians today claim to be filled with the Holy Spirit too, but they still live in a certain *culture*. You can be a born-again, Spirit-filled Christian but still . . . er . . . go to watch football matches and eat meat pies. The first Christians also lived in a particular culture, and our purpose today is to study that culture.'

'Yes', said Wade. 'When I was reading for this tutorial I was really interested to discover that different philosophers gathered groups of disciples around them, and some were itinerant teachers who went around the country areas preaching and performing "magic" tricks. That really puts Jesus of Nazareth in context.'

'But only Jesus taught the truth', maintained Frank. 'The rest, if they did exist, were only the devil's imposters.'

Wade raised his eyes toward the ceiling.

'In what ways do you think that Platonism and Neoplatonism could have helped Christians reflect on their beliefs and explain what they believed to others?' asked Derek.

'Christians must have been encouraged by the fact that educated men were stressing spiritual reality', commented Ruth musingly. 'Today we live in a society that places far greater emphasis on science and technology, and it is hard to get people to accept the existence of a spiritual world that they cannot see, touch, hear, taste or smell.'

'Yes, yes', agreed Derek eagerly. 'Anything else?'

'There is the issue of immortality of the soul', observed Christobel, not to be outshone by Ruth. 'That was a wonderfully radical concept for the times, and it heavily influenced later Christian thought. And we can also see a real tendency towards monotheism in Platonism and Neoplatonism. Instead of all those absolutely fascinating little local deities in pagan religions, Plato and Plotinus were pointing to a single, absolute, unchanging being: the Good or the One. Christians could have easily related that to their God.'

'And the philosophers generally placed a high degree of importance on people living good, upright lives', added Wade authoritatively. 'Plato was particularly concerned with the idea of a just society. The early Christians could have identified with that, in view of their Sermon-on-the-Mount teaching.'

We all nodded, and Ruth said that she thought that she had read somewhere that some of the philosophers' criticisms of traditional mythology were adopted by Christian writers in their attacks on paganism.

'They could have used that cave myth that Neville talked about', exclaimed Frank excitedly. 'They could have told the pagans that they were like the people chained up in the cave, but if they repented of their sins and asked Jesus to come into their hearts, they would be saved from the darkness and allowed into the light.'

'But,' he continued in an equally buoyant tone, 'I still reckon that the Christians weren't taken in by all that philosophy rubbish. After all, Plato's idea of God was of some kind of impersonal thing which didn't create the world or intervene in the affairs of men. We all know from the Old Testament that we have a Father God who created the world and everything in it. He also spoke through his prophets, looked after his chosen people (doing miracles like drying up the Red Sea so that the Israelites could escape from Egypt), and he punished them when they did wrong. Then he sent his only Son, Jesus Christ, to die for our sins on the cross, and the Holy Spirit to be our guide and comforter. We don't have to work our way to heaven through contemplation as those philosophers reckoned, just accept Jesus into our hearts. HALLELUJAH!'

'They're just faith statements', said Wade wearily. 'As far as creation is concerned, all societies have their different myths. I personally find Platonism and Neoplatonism more believable than the Genesis story, but that's just by the way. The point is, educated Christians *were* influenced by philosophy.'

'Did any of you . . . er . . . read what Christian writers in the second and third centuries thought about philosophy?' asked Derek.

'Oh, yes', replied Christobel at once. 'Except for conservative old Tertullian, who said "What has Athens to do with Jerusalem?" and practically ended up becoming a Pentecostal, they absolutely loved it. Justin Martyr explored various philosophical systems before converting to Christianity, and while he regarded Christianity as the complete revelation of reality, he did not reject his philosophical studies. In fact, he declared that as Christ was the divine Reason, Word, or Logos in human form, men like Socrates who had lived with reason in past ages were Christians, even though they appeared to be atheists. Isn't that a wonderful view of salvation? And Clement of Alexandria maintained that as "God is the cause of all good things", he must also be the cause of philosophy, and that "it educated the Greek world as the law did the Hebrews to *bring them to Christ*"! Origen encouraged his students to study secular philosophy because he believed that it would help them when they came to study the Bible, and Gregory the Wonderworker declared that secular philosophy *must* be studied to prepare the soul "to advance toward understanding things divine", and "true religion was impossible to one who did not philosophize". I think that's incredibly profound.'

Frank, however, wasn't convinced.

'The first disciples were ordinary fishermen and so on. They wouldn't have had much education and known about philosophy. And Jesus said that we have to have faith like little children. I reckon that later Christians stuffed up the Church with things like philosophy, making people count beads, penances, and all that kind of mumbo-jumbo that Roman Catholics believe that you can earn your way to heaven by.'

'Unfortunately, not everyone has a dramatic conversion experience and can have childlike faith straightaway', remarked Ruth quietly. 'Many people go through an intellectual struggle, as St Justin did.'

'But they still have to come to the point of accepting Jesus as Lord, or they're not saved', concluded Frank adamantly.

Wade looked as if he was about to burst.

Once again Derek rushed to the rescue.

'What other . . . er . . . aspects of Hellenistic culture do you think could have influenced Christianity?'

Christobel suggested art, because some early pictures and statues of Jesus bear an absolutely uncanny resemblance to those of the Greek god Apollo, and the Virgin Mary is portrayed awfully like the Egyptian goddess Isis.

Maureen snorted derisively.

'Well, if the silversmiths of Ephesus who got so upset because Paul was ruining their shrine-making businesses in Acts 19 had been entrepreneurs like my ex-husband, they would have pretty quickly turned to churning out silver crosses.'

'What I find significant is the amazing number of similarities between Christianity and Eastern mystery religions', asserted Wade. 'Concepts like rebirth, purification, salvation and immortality; initiatory rites like baptism; and customs like sacramental meals were certainly not unique to Christianity.'

Frank once again observed that one of the devil's favourite tactics is distorting the truth.

'I think that the point to . . . er . . . note is that Christianity did not . . . er . . . emerge into a religious and cultural vacuum', intervened Derek.

'Exactly', agreed Wade with an unusual degree of fervour. 'I didn't say that the mystery religions copied Christianity, or vice versa, but they clearly demonstrate parallel religious expressions of a shared cultural system. We are now faced with the challenge of interpreting Christianity in the light of culture in the late twentieth century – and I don't mean just that of Western society either. How can we make Christianity relevant to indigenous people, like the Australian Aborigines with their Dreamtime heritage? And the poor and oppressed people of the Third World? And what about issues like the nuclear arms race, the greenhouse effect, the liberation of women . . .?'

'But Jesus Christ is the same yesterday, today and forever', protested Frank. 'If we just stick to what he tells us in the Bible we can't go wrong. And he says in John 17 that we should be in the world but not of the world . . .'

For one awful moment I thought that all 1,022 pages of Wade's copy of *The Rise of Christianity* were going to collide with Frank's complacent smile. Fortunately, Wade restrained himself, although with noticeable effort.

'Thank you all for a most stimulating discussion', gasped Derek. 'Our time has almost run out, but I would like to leave you with a quotation from Everett Ferguson's *Backgrounds of Early Christianity* (1987: p 489). Er . . . Ferguson says that

> Popular religion was unable to hold the conviction of the educated, and philosophy was unable to reach the masses. Christianity successfully integrated a religious faith with a worldview and pattern of life that were philosophically defensible, if not "philosophical" in the strict sense.
> Nevertheless, the situation was not clear-cut. The pagan beliefs in demons, astrology, and magic were so resilient that they did not really die but were absorbed into the triumphant Christianity of a later age. Similarly, much of the traditional ritual survived in Christian ceremonies . . .'

'That's what I said earlier', interrupted Frank. 'The Roman Catholic Church stuffed things up. If we just stick to the New Testament, Acts 2:42 . . .'

Wade grabbed his books and strode out of the room.

As I was leaving, I heard Maureen ask Derek what the hell a 'parallel religious expression of a shared cultural system' meant. Thought how amazing it was that Christianity appealed to a wide cross-section of people in the Roman Empire, educated and uneducated, from all different kinds of backgrounds. And it still does today—if our tutorial group is anything to go by!

# WEEK·SEVEN
## Orthodoxy versus heresy

Today we were supposed to look at a weird religious movement/sect/phenomenon called Gnosticism, and one of its main opponents in the late second century, Bishop Irenaeus of Lyons. Had a bit of trouble working out exactly what Gnosticism was, because historians can't seem to agree on whether it existed before Christianity or not, and whether it influenced the New Testament. Basically, however, the term is derived from the Greek word for knowledge. Gnostics seem to have believed that they possessed some kind of secret revelation.

Christobel arrived wearing a tight red miniskirt, black high-heeled thigh-length leather boots, and a red and black striped blazer with huge silver buttons. She announced that in honour of the occasion she was wearing her 'Gnostic' perfume. It's actually called Secret Knowledge. She reached over Neville and dabbed some on Kirsty's wrist. Also offered some to Ruth and Maureen but fortunately they declined it. I thought it was a bit strong – anything but 'secret'.

That over and done with, Derek asked us what we thought of Gnosticism.

Christobel immediately said that it was absolutely fascinating.

'If I had lived in the second century I'm absolutely sure

that I might have been a Gnostic too, for I simply can't resist those wonderful mystical insights into how we can liberate our spirits from the prisons which are our bodies and soar through the *pleroma* . . .'

Christobel's voice trailed off ecstatically, interrupted at the end by a loud sneeze from Neville.

'From what I read, it sounded stupid', commented Maureen caustically. 'Even worse than that philosophy stuff we studied last week.'

'Gnosticism was a syncretistic, eclectic phenomenon which combined aspects of philosophy with elements of various Eastern religions, including Judaism and Christianity', observed Wade in his knowledgeable way.

'It certainly wasn't what I call Christian', maintained Maureen. 'The God of the Old Testament wasn't the supreme God but some kind of evil power, and Jesus didn't have a real human body or really suffer and die . . .'

'But that's the most exciting thing about Gnosticism!' exclaimed Christobel. 'The Gnostics grappled with deep moral and intellectual problems that still trouble people today. How could a supposedly good God create a world which is so full of evil and suffering? And how could an omnipotent, omnipresent divine being become a mere man?'

Thought Neville was going to sneeze again, but he managed to suppress it.

'Of course, the Gnostics answered those questions by believing in a single, absolute, and unknowable God, the God that Paul talked about in Acts 17', asserted Wade. 'It sent Christ as a heavenly messenger to help those humans who had divine sparks within them ascend past the evil powers (such as the Jewish God) which created and still control the world.'

'Yes, and isn't that a wonderful answer to the problem of theodicy?' enthused Christobel. 'It was frightfully popular in the second century.'

'What's theodicy?' asked Kirsty with an embarrassed flush.

While Derek was explaining that it referred to theories about God and the existence of evil, Neville asked me in a whisper if he could borrow a hanky.

'However,' continued Christobel enthusiastically, while I hunted around in my pockets for a clean one, 'most of all I simply adored reading about Marcion. He wasn't exactly a Gnostic, but, like me, he absolutely couldn't accept that the harsh, vindictive God of the Old Testament was the God of love revealed by Jesus Christ.'

'He also rejected much of the New Testament', put in Wade. 'All but Luke's gospel and the Pauline epistles (excluding pastorals). And he subjected them to pretty thorough editing too.'

'Now that's taking biblical exegesis too far', said Maureen critically. 'Not that I like everything in the Bible, but I don't go chopping things out just because they don't suit me. Can't blame ordinary Christians for getting upset.'

Neville sneezed twice.

'How did Irenaeus respond to that kind of challenge?' intervened Derek.

Ruth pondered this question thoughtfully.

'Unlike Marcion he had a high regard for the Old Testament and strongly believed in its relevance for Christians', she said. 'He portrayed our Lord as the new Adam through whom God rehabilitated the divine plan for salvation, which had been interrupted by the first Adam's fall. I think that Irenaeus was also one of the first Christian writers to assert the authority of the New Testament writings and establish a canon, a list of authentic Scriptures . . .'

'But it wasn't exactly the same as the one in use today', interrupted Wade. 'He left out Philemon, Hebrews, James, 2 Peter, 3 John, and Jude; and he included another early writing called the Shepherd of Hermas. And his explanation for why there are only four true gospels is positively ludicrous: that there are four regions of the world, four winds, and four faces on cherubim. How any intelligent person could be expected to swallow that, even in the second century, beats me.'

Neville sneezed again.

'Didn't Irenaeus also establish a Rule of Faith, sort of like a creed to help Christians know what is really true?' ventured Kirsty.

'But, as Pontius Pilate so perceptively commented, what is truth?' said Wade, throwing his hands in the air.

'According to Irenaeus, the teaching of Jesus and the apostles recorded in the Bible and preserved by the mainstream Church', replied Ruth, smiling at Kirsty. 'And this passage in his *Against Heresies* certainly sounds very much like a creed:

The Church, although scattered throughout the earth to its very limits, received from the Apostles and their disciples this faith: There is one God, the Father almighty "who made heaven and earth and the sea and all they contain" (Acts 4:24; 14:15). (We believe) in one Christ Jesus, the Son of God, who became flesh for our salvation, and in the Holy Spirit who announced God's plan through the Prophets: his coming, his birth from the Virgin, his passion and resurrection from the dead, the ascension in the flesh to Heaven of his beloved Jesus Christ our Lord and his return from Heaven in the glory of the Father to gather all things and to raise in the flesh the entire human race so that to Christ Jesus, our Lord and God, Saviour and King, according to the good pleasure of the invisible Father, "every knee must bend in the heavens and on earth and under the earth and every tongue confess him" (Philippians 2:10, 11).'

'But how do we know that is the truth?' pursued Wade doggedly. 'To me, that passage simply indicates that Irenaeus was desperately trying to counter the Gnostics by reducing Christianity to a fixed set of beliefs, a closed system with no room for the kind of speculative inquiry that the Gnostics excelled at.'

Neville sneezed three times and asked if he could borrow another hanky.

'Ireneaus believed that it was the truth because it was taught by churches, like the one in Rome, which had been established by the apostles and kept to their teaching', remarked Ruth with unruffled composure. 'He particularly cited the Roman church. Now, I know that there has been considerable debate over whether or not he advocated the primacy of Rome, but regardless of the truth about that, I think that it is very important to realize that he was personally acquainted with St Polycarp, bishop of Smyrna, who had known St John the "beloved disciple", and other people who had been eyewitnesses of our Lord's earthly ministry. Irenaeus therefore had a direct link with the apostolic age, and would have been in a far better position to know what Christian teaching was authentic and what wasn't than people like Marcion.'

'But he was only a child when he supposedly met Polycarp', objected Wade, 'and, anyway, all through the gospel accounts we can see that the disciples continually misunderstood Jesus' teaching and ministry . . .'

'Until they were filled with the Holy Spirit and guided into all truth', finished Frank jubilantly, coming into the room in time to hear Wade's last statement.

Wade glared at him.

'Er. . . Frank, we have just been discussing Bishop Irenaeus's reactions to Gnosticism', said Derek uneasily.

'Sorry I'm late', apologized Frank in a cheerfully unrepentant tone. 'I had to exorcise my car.'

'What on earth was wrong with it?' asked Maureen bluntly. 'It stopped a couple of kilometres away. I think that the devil was trying to prevent me getting here.'

'And you really fixed it through prayer?' exclaimed Kirsty, visibly impressed.

'Oh, well, it had actually run out of petrol,' admitted Frank rather bashfully, 'but just after I prayed a Christian sister stopped and gave me a lift to the nearest petrol station', he added on a defiant note.

'To get back to the point of this discussion,' began Wade coldly, 'Gnostic Christianity shows how well some Christians adapted their beliefs and practices to the prevailing Hellenistic culture.'

Neville got out an inhaler.

'And some other stuffy, intolerant Christians couldn't accept that people could seek God in a way that was different from theirs, and so they ruthlessly persecuted the poor Gnostics', concluded Christobel with vigour. 'Thank goodness all those wonderful Gnostic texts were discovered at Nag Hammadi in 1945, so that we can now see that the kind of Christianity established by sexist, authoritarian bishops like Irenaeus wasn't the only kind in existence in the first centuries of the common era.'

'But I thought there was a need to sort of define what Christianity really was so that new converts didn't get sort of led astray', said Kirsty, looking troubled.

'But what is truth?' responded Wade airily.

'And how can anyone adequately define Christianity?' continued Christobel, eyes flashing. 'I am absolutely sure that I can get closer to God through mystical contemplation than through parroting the creeds drawn up by the male-dominated mainstream churches, and I defy anyone to prove me wrong!'

No one dared make the attempt.

'Well, what struck me when I was reading for this tutorial,' declared Maureen at last, 'was how sensible and believable mainstream Christianity seems to be in comparison with all this Gnostic stuff. Listen to this. It doesn't make sense.

> Secundus says that there is a first Ogdoad, a right-hand and a left-hand Tetrad, as he would have them called, one light, the other darkness; and the Power that fell away and suffered lack was not begotten of the thirty Aeons, but of their fruits . . . There is a certain Proarche before all things, beyond any thought or speech or name, whom I call Monotes; with this Monotes is another Power whom I call Henotes.

'Fancy reading that out in church on Sunday morning! And there's a whole lot more, because all of the Gnostic groups seem to have had different beliefs and hated each other as much as they hated normal Christians. I reckon they got carried away with a lot of rubbish, and that's what Irenaeus thought too:

> Iu, iu, and pheu, pheu! Truly we may utter these exclamations from tragedy at such bold invention of ridiculous nomenclature, and at the audacity that made up these names without blushing.

'Then he goes on, mimicking the Gnostics:

> There is a royal Proarch above all thought, a Power above all substance, indefinitely extended. Since this is the Power

which I call the Gourd, there is with it the Power which I call Superemptiness. This Gourd and Superemptiness, being one, emitted, yet did not emit, the fruit, visible, edible and delicious, which is known to language as the Cucumber. With this Cucumber there is a Power of like quality with it, which I call the Melon. These Powers, the Gourd, Superemptiness, the Cucumber and the Melon, sent forth the remaining crowd of the delirious Melons of Valentinus.

'Valentinus was one of the Gnostic teachers and, like the rest of them, seems to have needed a good dose of antacid.'

At this point Neville was overcome by another fit of sneezing and rushed out of the room.

'The poor boy must be getting a cold', said Christobel in a concerned voice. 'I'll just run after him and offer him a throat lozenge. What a good thing I have some in my bag.'

Off she went, as fast as her high heels could carry her, and sounds of sneezing and running could be heard receding down the corridor.

'More like an overdose of "Gnosis" than a cold, if you ask me', snorted Maureen. 'Enough to make anyone ill.'

It was funny that she should say that, because I could feel another one of my sinus headaches coming on.

Fortunately, Derek said that it was time to finish up.

While the rest of us got up and collected our books and papers, Kirsty remained seated, lost in thought.

'It is awfully difficult to work out what is the truth, isn't it?' she said pensively.

I confessed that I am not very adventurous spiritually and just accept the teaching of the mainstream Church.

'Think about it, pray about it, and listen to your conscience, dear', advised Ruth gently.

'And your common sense!' added Maureen astringently.

# Week·Eight

## The role of women

Christobel's turn to lead the group. Arrived to find the room decked with banners left over from a Movement for the Ordination of Women rally: GALATIANS 3:28; WE WILL NOT BE MOVED; WOMEN IN, SEXIST PIGS OUT; and so on. It was really a bit daunting. As a member of the male sex I resolved to keep a very low profile.

Christobel, however, had other ideas. I discovered later that she used to be chief cheerleader at a certain prestigious Anglican girls school.

'Who were healed and forgiven by Jesus?' she cried, eyes sparkling brightly.

Silence as we racked our brains, trying to recall the various healing miracles in the gospels.

'Women?' ventured Ruth at last.

'WOMEN!!!' affirmed Christobel at the top of her voice. 'Who were taught by Jesus?'

'Women?' we suggested feebly.

'WOMEN!!!' shouted Christobel. 'Who travelled with Jesus around the countryside, joining his group of itinerant followers?'

'Women', we chorused, catching on quite well.

And so it went on.

Christobel: 'Who supported Jesus' ministry in many practical ways?'

Rest of us: 'Women!'

Christobel: (triumphantly) 'Who DIDN'T run away from the cross?

R.O.U.: 'Women!'

Christobel: (even more triumphantly) 'And who were the first people to see the risen Lord?'

Kirsty: (caught off guard) 'Peter and John!'

Christobel: (utilizing maximum vocal capacity) 'WOMEN!!!'

She then fixed her eyes sternly on Derek, Frank, Wade, Neville and me.

'And who were apostles, prophets, deacons, community leaders and missionaries in the earliest churches?'

Frank sat with his face impassive and his arms crossed.

'Women', the rest of us squeaked.

'Who did charitable work, taught, preached and prophesied?'

'Women', we squeaked again.

'And what eventually happened to them?' finished Christobel bitterly. 'They were turned into widows.'

Had to admit that this seemed a bit unfair.

'There is, of course, considerable . . . er . . . debate about women's orders in the early Church', said Derek in a worried voice. 'However, Ignatius's correspondence to Polycarp at the turn of the century does seems to imply that "widows" was a technical term for women who devoted themselves to chastity and our Lord's work.'

'And unmarried virgins who joined them were called widows too', asserted Wade knowledgeably. 'Moreover, Clement of Alexandria spoke of a female diaconate, the *Apostolic Tradition* (*c* .170 to 236) describes a ceremony for laying hands on deaconesses, and the *Didascalia Apostolorum* (early third century) recounts some of the duties of a deaconess.'

'Assisting at baptisms of women, instructing female catechumens, and visiting and attending to the needs of the sick', muttered Christobel crossly.

'And I suppose that they were also supposed to keep celibate, pray constantly, and be totally loving, generous, and hospitable', added Maureen sarcastically. 'How many did the Church have – two?'

'Their duties might seem arduous to us, but they were given freedom from family cares and responsibilities which were quite considerable in those days', pointed out Ruth.

'But they were squeezed out of preaching, teaching and participation in liturgical worship by male chauvinist pig bishops!' responded Christobel swiftly, her eyes flashing with militant zeal. 'And in the fifth and sixth centuries horrid church councils actually ordered that the ordination of deaconesses cease altogether.'

Frank thought this over.

'Ah', he said at last. 'I think that you must be forgetting, Christobel, that the apostle Paul said: "Women should remain silent in the churches. They are not allowed to speak, but must be in submission" (1 Corinthians 14:34), and "I do not permit a woman to teach or to have authority over a man" (1 Timothy 2:12).'

'That absolutely appalling passage in Corinthians was clearly inserted into Paul's letter by some pompous male scribe,' seethed Christobel, 'and no biblical scholar or theologian worth his or her stipend still believes that the pastoral epistles were actually written by Paul. It's quite obvious that they were composed at the end of the century, when an authoritarian male hierarchy was coming into existence, far removed from the Jesus tradition and Paul's second-generation version of Christianity.'

'Well, I don't agree with that, and, anyway, the Bible makes it very clear that God is our *Father* and Jesus Christ is his *Son*, and all Jesus' disciples were male, and Adam was created first', struck back Frank.

'It is totally inappropriate to ascribe our human and sexual limitations to God', said Wade in a lofty tone. 'He/she far transcends them. And there are two versions of the Genesis creation myth. Although Genesis 2 certainly speaks of Adam being created first, Genesis 1 gives no hint of that, but declares that *both* male and female were created in the image of God.'

Christobel absolutely agreed.

'I fully support movements for the ordination of women', went on Wade, in a faintly patronizing way. 'Basically, it's a cultural and not a theological issue. Although the New Testament writers perceived that "in Christ there is neither Jew nor Greek, slave nor free, male nor female, for you are all one in Christ Jesus", they could not break free from first-century prejudices against women and slaves. It took Christians 1,800 years to realize that slavery was incompatible with Jesus' teaching, and sadly it looks like taking more than 2,000 years for many churches to accept that the same is true with regard to the subordination of women.'

'Where does the Catholic Church stand on women's rights now?' asked Maureen abruptly.

'The Vatican is still holding out against female priests, but there are many Catholic women, including me, who would be ordained tomorrow if we got the chance', replied Ruth. 'I can't see it happening for a while though.'

Christobel was struck by a sudden thought.

'Forget about female priests', she said with a dazed look on her face. 'What we really need is a FEMALE POPE!'

'Yes,' agreed Kirsty enthusiastically, 'someone like Mother Teresa'.

'She'd be too busy being a Christian to be the pope', said Wade with a sarcastic laugh.

'All she'd have to do would be to make policy decisions and celebrate mass occasionally', cried Christobel, refusing to be put off. 'The cardinesses could handle all the routine administrative stuff.'

'Well, I'd like someone who'd been a mother to be the pope', said Maureen. 'And then one thing would be certain: she'd legalize artificial contraception in her first ten minutes in office. And there's another special thing about mothers', continued Maureen forcefully. 'It came to me one day last year when I'd just finished typing my son's thesis and sewing the 1,010th sequin on my youngest daughter's ballet costume. Every significant person in history has had a mother – INCLUDING JESUS CHRIST!'

We pondered over this profound truth in silence for a few moments.

'But if a lady pope was married, what would her husband do and what would he be called?' asked Kirsty at last. 'Would it be sort of like the Queen and Prince Philip?'

'I suppose it would be simpler if she was a widow', conceded Maureen. (*I think that she was talking about the female pope, not Queen Elizabeth.*) 'Husbands are useless anyway.'

'Er . . . to return to our topic for today,' began Derek feebly, 'many books have been written recently about the role of women in the early Church. It does seem possible that their role was quite . . . er . . . considerable at first but declined somewhat later. Can you think of any reasons why this could have . . . er. . . occurred?'

'Male chauvinist pig bishops!' stated Christobel angrily.

Wade thumped the table with his fist.

'It is one of the great tragedies of Christianity that while Jesus upheld the marginalized and challenged the established norms, his followers soon began to accommodate prevailing social customs. Perhaps they were trying to prove to hostile authorities that they did not pose a threat to the existing social order, or win converts from the wealthier, more conservative classes. In any case, the results were the same. Slaves were told to obey their masters and women were told to obey their husbands.'

Christobel absolutely agreed.

'I seem to remember that women also had a fairly prominent role in some heretical Gnostic and Montanist groups', said Ruth pensively. 'A backlash against them could have contributed to the limiting of women's roles in the mainstream Church.'

'Yes', agreed Derek. 'That's a good point.'

'Well, I'd rather be a Gnostic than a mainstream Christian any day', declared Christobel in an intransigent tone.

'Er . . . you know that most Gnostic groups were not so much pro-women as anti-sexual?' ventured Derek bravely. 'But, in any case, perhaps we should now consider the portrayal of women in patristic literature.'

'Tertullian was clearly an old conservative stick-in-the-mud with a strong chauvinistic streak, but Clement of Alexandria wasn't too bad', acknowledged Christobel grudgingly. 'He at least recognized that not everyone had to be celibate to be a Christian.'

'According to Susanne Heine's book *Women and Early Christianity: Are the Feminist Scholars Right?*, Tertullian wasn't really as negative toward women as some feminist writers have claimed, and Clement of Alexandria wasn't quite as positive', responded Ruth gently. 'I agree with Elizabeth Clark that the Church Fathers seem to have had a very ambivalent attitude towards women. As she says in *Women in the Early Church* (p 15), the Fathers wrote that

> Women were God's creation, his good gift to men – and the curse of the world. They were weak in both mind and character – and displayed dauntless courage, undertook prodigious feats of scholarship. Vain, deceitful, brimming with lust – they led men to Christ, fled sexual encounter, wavered not at the executioner's threats, adorned themselves with sackcloth and ashes . . .'

'Thank you, Ruth, for that quotation', said Derek, looking pleased. 'If no one has anything else to say, we can perhaps conclude on that note. And, as I am sure you are all aware, this is our last meeting for the term. I will . . . er . . . look forward to seeing you in two weeks' time.'

On the way out we discussed how we intended to spend the mid-semester break.

Christobel casually announced that she was going to a Christian feminists' theological conference, and she would then go on to France to unwind for a week.

Wade rather smugly disclosed that, as it was going to be school holidays, he would mind his children while his partner worked, thus demonstrating once again his support for women's liberation.

Kirsty excitedly confided that she was going home to the farm (mother, father, older brother, two younger sisters, three dogs, two cats, horse called Ginger, pet bantam, lamb, and I forget how many baby calves).

When pressed, Ruth revealed that she was heading off to a prayer retreat.

Neville stuttered that he hoped to do some walking (he

whispered to me that he felt closest to God in the countryside), and Maureen explained in great detail how busy she would be preparing for her eldest daughter's wedding. By the sound of things, she'd be snowed under by cream puffs and white tulle ('The things a mother has got to do . . .').

Frank exuberantly declared that members of his Christian fellowship had just finished a three-week evangelism course. They planned to put their teaching into practice by doorknocking a thousand homes in their area and adjoining suburbs. Frank was rostered to do 425, which he expected would keep him pretty busy, as he was prepared to spend time counselling anyone who needed help.

And me? I just thought that I'd better get on with writing all the essays that will be due next term!

# WEEK·NINE

## The triumph of Christianity?

First tutorial for the new term. Derek welcomed us back and said that today we would be looking at a great turning point in history. In 312 Constantine invaded Italy, won a surprisingly easy victory over his rival Maxentius at the Milvian Bridge near Rome, and became emperor of the western half of the Roman Empire. In 324 he took control of the whole empire. According to contemporary Christian historians, Lactantius and Eusebius, he attributed his success to the favour of the Christian God, which had been promised to him in a vision. Derek was sure that we had all read about this extremely important time in the history of Christianity.

Maureen said that actually she hadn't had time to do any reading because of her daughter's wedding last Saturday, but she'd brought us each a piece of wedding cake. It really was very nice. She'd made it and iced it herself.

After an interval in which the wedding was discussed and the cake consumed, Derek rather anxiously looked at his watch and suggested that we consider the question: How did Constantine's patronage of Christianity affect the Church?

Kirsty was the first to attempt an answer.

'It must have been wonderful when the persecutions ended and the emperor gave so many gifts to Christians. He built lots of churches, and he had new copies of the Bible made, and he gave heaps of money to be distributed to the poor, and he let the bishop of Rome have the Lateran Palace . . .'

'I reckon that's when the Church started getting corrupt', interrupted Frank. 'All the property and wealth Constantine gave bishops went right against Jesus' teaching that "it is easier for a camel to go through the eye of a needle than for a rich man to enter the kingdom of heaven". And it's downright sinful the way churches still waste money on property when they should be concentrating on saving souls. I'm proud to say that my Prayer, Praise and Holy Power group meets in people's homes, just as the first Christians did, instead of squandering money on bricks and mortar.'

'Oh, I don't object to church buildings', responded Christobel, waving her arms around in an airy gesture. 'Stained-glass windows and organ music are so awfully conducive to proper worship. But I do think that it was a pity that Constantine gave so much extra status to pompous male bishops. They ended up having practically the same power as secular magistrates, access to the imperial court and all that kind of thing, which must have reinforced sexist male values at the expense of women's rights. And Constantine was an absolute autocrat and murdered half his family, which I think was frightfully un-Christian.'

'But typical of a Roman emperor', observed Maureen in her forthright way. 'I can understand Christians carrying on after the persecutions as though Constantine was the greatest thing since sliced bread, but it seems to me pretty obvious that Christian Roman Emperor is a contradiction in terms. We all know that politicians are arrogant, power-hungry egomaniacs, but at least today they've got to go through a more or less democratic process to get elected, and they've got journalists forever yapping at their heels, watching everything they do. Roman emperors didn't have to worry about those sorts of restrictions, and as my old mother used to say, "all power corrupts and absolute power corrupts absolutely".'

'Constantine wasn't actually baptized until just before his death', remarked Ruth in a thoughtful tone. 'But he did seem to consider himself a Christian. According to Eusebius, he even referred to himself once as a bishop ordained by God to care for people outside the Church. And he passed legislation which shows Christian influence, such as the banning of crucifixion and branding on the face.'

'But criminals could still be forced to drink molten lead,' objected Christobel, 'which I think was absolutely horrid, and, anyway, Constantine had no right to call himself a bishop and meddle in church affairs. I fail to see why he had to call that awful Council of Nicaea and force Christian bishops to clarify their beliefs and exile the poor heretics.'

'So you . . . er . . . feel that Constantine's conversion was not necessarily a good thing for the Church?' said Derek.

Christobel, Maureen and Frank unhesitatingly said yes.

'What do you mean by "conversion"?' Wade asked Derek in a superior tone. 'I totally agree with Alistair Kee's assessment (in his book *Constantine Versus Christ*) that Constantine's so-called conversion was more like a pragmatic political decision to change divine patronage and ally himself to the god of the Christians. This decision must have seemed justified by the victory at the Milvian Bridge, and Constantine then *used* Christianity to help legitimize his rule and unify the empire.'

Wade will sure make a good preacher. He speaks with such authority and never seems lost for words.

'Unfortunately, the Christians who had successfully endured persecution fell over themselves in their hurry to thank and praise their supposed benefactor', he continued eloquently, 'little realizing that he posed a far greater threat to the Church than conservative pagan emperors like Decius and Diocletian. This can be seen in the work of the Christian historian Eusebius, for example. The life, ministry and death of Jesus of Nazareth pale into insignificance beside the glorious power, wealth and victories of the emperor. Of course, the Church didn't totally reject Jesus in favour of Constantine, but gradually and insidiously the values of Constantine *replaced* the values of Christ – wealth, secular power and military might instead of poverty, humility and service. Artists portrayed Christ sitting on a heavenly throne surrounded by wealth, power and privilege, just like the emperor, and the organization of the Church modelled itself on the organization of the State. Tragically, it served (and in many cases continues to serve) the interests of the ruling classes rather than the oppressed and marginalized who were the main targets of Jesus' ministry.'

Christobel absolutely agreed.

'And when Constantine made Christianity fashionable, lots of pagans came into the Church who weren't properly converted', added Frank, 'and they brought with them priests and altars and incense and stuff from pagan religions that are totally unbiblical.'

'Weren't there priests and altars and incense in Old Testament times?' interjected Maureen.

'But in the New Testament the word "priest" is only used in relation to the Jewish priests, our high priest Jesus (Hebrews 4:14), and the "royal priesthood" of all believers (1 Peter 2:9)', argued Frank.

'I take Frank's point that the Church did change considerably in the fourth century, as Christianity moved from being . . . er . . . a persecuted minority religion to being the dominant religion of the empire', conceded Derek. 'And certainly Constantine was . . . er . . . primarily responsible for this.'

'I sometimes feel a bit sorry for him though', said Ruth meekly. 'He seems to get blamed for everything that went wrong in the Church, but the Church had begun to acquire property before he came to power, and a strong ecclesiastical hierarchy had already come into existence.'

'But it was in his time that the Church really became established and institutionalized,' maintained Wade, 'and hence the tool of the ruling classes.'

'What could you find out about Constantine's successors?' said Derek.

Felt tempted to say that they seemed a fairly mediocre lot, but Wade got in before me and declared that by and large they followed Constantine's policies.

'Except for poor Julian, who became emperor in 361', said Christobel sympathetically. 'He was absolutely fascinated by classical Greek culture and tried to restore pagan religion, but he only ruled for two years before dying in battle.'

'HOORAY!' exclaimed Frank exuberantly. 'So much for his old pagan gods! Ha-ha-ha!'

Christobel cast him a reproachful look.

'Well, I absolutely adore classical Greek culture too, and I think it was frightfully horrid the way fundamentalist Christians went around vandalizing wonderful pagan statues and temples. And it was totally unnecessary for Emperor Theodosius I to ban pagan sacrifices and rites in 391 . . .'

'PRAISE THE LORD!' cried Frank, punching the air with his fist. 'Let the pagans have a taste of the treatment they'd been handing out to Christians! Send them to the arena!'

'They probably were,' snapped Christobel, 'but if you think people should be converted to Christianity through torture you've forgotten large chunks of your precious Bible. I think that it's terribly tragic that the victims of intolerance at the beginning of the century were the perpetrators of it at the end. It makes me ashamed to be a Christian!'

Maureen said that it stuck in her gullet too, and Wade remarked that it showed the influence of Constantine's values (not Christ's) and that they were still around today.

'To . . . er . . . return to Church-State relations', said Derek quickly, 'did any of you read about St Ambrose? Kirsty, Michael, and Neville, would you . . . er . . . like a chance to speak?'

We all looked blank and finally Ruth quietly intervened.

'He was bishop of Milan in the latter half of the fourth century, wasn't he? I read that he was involved in a confrontation with the Dowager Empress Justina. She demanded that a church be made available for the use of the Arian Christians in her entourage, but St Ambrose regarded them as heretics and refused to give in to her demands. As tension mounted and a showdown seemed imminent, Ambrose preached sermons about Eve and Jezebel and wrote a letter to his sister. I think I can find it in Stevenson's collection of documents . . .'

She flicked through the pages of *Creeds, Councils and Controversies.*

'Yes, here it is, page 128:

'At last the command was given: Surrender the basilica. My reply was, it is not lawful for me to surrender it, nor advantageous for you, Sir, to receive it. By no right can you violate the house of a private person, and do you think that the house of God may be taken away? It is asserted that everything is lawful for the Emperor, that all things are his. My answer is: Do not, O Emperor, lay on yourself the burden of such a thought as that you have any imperial power over those things which belong to God. It is written: "The things which are God's to God, those which are Caesar's to Caesar." The palaces belong to the Emperor, the churches to the Bishop.'

Pretty strong stuff! And, according to Ruth, Ambrose eventually got his way.

'Pompous, intolerant, chauvinistic old twit', muttered Christobel with a contemptuous sniff.

Derek then said that Ambrose had an even greater victory over Theodosius. In 390 there were riots in Thessalonica and one of the emperor's officials was killed. Theodosius responded by inviting the inhabitants of Thessalonica to an amphitheatre to see a special show. When everyone was seated, soldiers moved in. It has been estimated that within three hours 7,000 men, women and children were killed.

That sent Maureen right off about the arrogance and callousness of emperors, and she said that for the life of her she couldn't see what difference being a Christian made to them.

'The . . . er . . . difference was that Ambrose excommunicated the emperor', responded Derek, when he could eventually get a word in. 'To put it mildly, Roman emperors were not . . . er . . . used to being excommunicated. Theodosius tried to wriggle out of it by comparing himself to King David, who, in spite of being an adulterer and a murderer, was reinstated to divine favour, but Ambrose held firm and insisted that he publicly repent.'

'So the Church ended the century triumphant', I unwisely commented.

'Ambrose certainly . . . er . . . upheld the Church's authority over the emperor in ecclesiastical matters,' replied Derek hesitatingly, 'but unfortunately the exact relationship between Church and State (and which power was ultimately subordinate to the other) remained a very contentious issue, especially in the medieval period.'

'I think they should be completely separate', said Maureen forcefully.

Christobel agreed that the State should not interfere in any way in the affairs of Christian denominations (except to provide funds for their schools), but she felt that the Church as a whole could become more politicized.

'It should be in the vanguard of political reform,' thundered Wade, 'upholding the rights of the marginalized, fighting for the preservation of the natural resources God has blessed us with, and working for international peace and goodwill. And I am not just talking about church leaders, either. Instead of merely going to church for an hour on Sunday, singing a few nice hymns, hearing a pious sermon, and praying a brief prayer for the well-being of the nation before going home to a roast dinner, we should be out on the streets marching for peace and disarmament, greater help for the unemployed, the disabled, the environment . . .'

'I ABSOLUTELY agree!' cried Christobel passionately. 'ONWARD, CHRISTIAN SOLDIERS!!!'

'Well, I'm afraid I've got to dash off to an appointment with my chiropodist', said Maureen. 'No good me doing any marching until my corns are fixed.'

This reminded Derek that our time together had expired.

'Er . . . we will meet again next week to consider early Christian attitudes to war and violence,' he said in a rather depressed voice.

'Great!' said Wade. 'I can't wait.'

'Have you ever been in a street march?' Kirsty whispered to me as we were leaving.

Had to confess I hadn't. I don't really think I can be very 'politicized'.

Frank came up behind us.

'It's REVIVAL we need, not political reform', he asserted confidently. 'Don't you worry about politics, Kirsty, just pray for the THIRD WAVE and the SECOND COMING.'

Poor Kirsty looked a bit dazed.

'But do you think if Jesus came again soon he would *like* to find me involved in a street march? I know my mum wouldn't.'

'I think it would depend on the issue', replied Ruth soothingly.

'Well, you could never go wrong protesting against war and violence!' interjected Christobel firmly.

More about that next week!

# WEEK·TEN

## Christian attitudes to war and violence

Funny weather today. Unusually warm and humid, with a storm brewing. To make matters worse, the university heating system had gone into overdrive just as we were gathering to discuss the writings of Ambrose of Milan (as quoted by Louis Swift in *The Early Fathers on War and Military Service*). Derek, looking rather hot and hassled, said that we had better begin by briefly reviewing earlier Christian attitudes to war and violence.

'It's frightfully obvious that *true* Christians can't be anything other than pacifists', proclaimed Christobel.

Wade inclined his head.

'Jesus reportedly said in the Sermon on the Mount: "Blessed are the peacemakers, for they will be called children of God". Moreover, "if someone strikes you on the right cheek, turn to him your other also . . ." How more pacifistic can you get?'

'And I suppose Jesus set us an example by suffering and dying himself', observed Maureen fair-mindedly. 'But I wish that he'd been more assertive and leapt down from the cross and zapped his enemies dead. Can't anyone open a window?'

Neville and I tried our best but all the windows seemed to be jammed shut.

'Jesus could have instigated a violent revolt against Rome and the Jewish authorities if he had shared the corrupt values of the secular world', exclaimed Wade. 'However, he had a far different set of values, which the early Christians tried to adopt. As Justin Martyr commented in the second century: "We who were filled with war, mutual slaughter, and every other form of evil have everywhere transformed our instruments of war, fashioning our swords into ploughshares and our spears into farm tools. We are now cultivators of piety, justice, generosity, faith and the hope which comes from the Father through him who was crucified . . ."'

'Tertullian and Origen said much the same kind of thing in the third century', cried Christobel triumphantly. 'I don't usually have much time for Tertullian, but in his book *Against the Jews* he distinguished the New Law from the Old:

For the practice of the Old Law was to avenge itself with the sword, to take an eye for an eye and to repay injury for injury. But the practice of the New Law was to focus on clemency and to turn bloodthirsty swords and lances to peaceful uses and to change the warlike acts against rivals and enemies into the peaceful pursuits of ploughing and farming the land.

'And Origen declared:

We have come in response to Jesus' commands to beat into ploughshares the rational swords of conflict and arrogance and to change into pruning hooks those spears that we used to fight with. For we no longer take up the sword against any nation, nor do we learn the art of war anymore . . . We have become sons of peace through Jesus our leader . . .'

'Just think,' urged Wade, his voice ringing with passionate conviction, 'what the world would be like if we all lived according to the Sermon on the Mount. There'd be no more need for armed forces, and governments could pour all the money they'd save into social welfare projects . . .'

'Ah, but I'm afraid that we live in a sinful world', pointed out Frank, 'and the people of God are continually confronted by evil forces. However (PRAISE THE LORD!) God is a holy and righteous God who punishes evil and comes to the aid of his chosen ones. Sometimes he does this through direct intervention, like when he set up an ambush to defeat the men of Ammon and Moab when they invaded Judah when Jehoshaphat was king, and sometimes he commands his people to fight, like when he ordered Joshua to invade the land of Canaan and kill all its inhabitants.'

'I hardly think those pre-Christian stories of dubious historical and ethical value have any bearing on our topic today', said Wade crushingly.

Christobel agreed that they were absolutely incompatible with the loving God revealed by Jesus Christ and she totally disregarded them.

'But God doesn't love evil,' struck back Frank, 'and it says in Revelation that Jesus will come again as a conquering warrior and defeat all the forces of the devil. Revelation 19: "I saw heaven standing open and there before me was a white horse, whose rider is called Faithful and True. With justice he judges and makes war. His eyes are like blazing fire, and on his head are many crowns."'

There certainly was a blazing gleam in Frank's eyes, but Wade was not impressed.

'Imagery borrowed from Jewish apocalyptic writings', he said sweepingly, 'and not meant to be taken literally. It does not alter the fact that before Constantine Christians *were* pacifists.'

'I know that early Christian writings are predominantly

pacifistic in tone, if they address the issues of war and violence at all', remarked Ruth, her brows furrowed in concentration, 'but there must have been *some* Christians in the imperial army, because Diocletian began his persecution by trying to remove them!'

Derek said that was a very interesting point.

'Perhaps we could consider for a moment the attitude of Christians to the imperial State', he went on, wiping the sweat from his brow.

'Weren't they supposed to sort of submit to the ruling authorities?' asked Kirsty shyly.

'Romans 13: "Everyone must submit himself to the governing authorities, for there is no authority except that which God has established"', quoted Frank with a pleased look.

'I wouldn't have submitted to the State, because I think the State stank', said Maureen intransigently.

We all laughed.

'Of course, Christians couldn't go along with the idolatry demanded by some Roman emperors, and it must have been difficult to respect the State in times of persecution, but I suspect that apart from that many Christians would have considered themselves good, loyal citizens of the empire', maintained Ruth quietly.

'There was no reason why they couldn't *pray* for the well-being of the empire', conceded Christobel, fanning herself with some papers. 'In fact, Origen said that they did. Listen to this (she produced a copy of A *New Eusebius*):

> While others fight, Christians also should be fighting as priests and worshippers of God, keeping their right hands pure and by their prayers to God striving for those who fight in a righteous cause and for the emperor who reigns

righteously . . . Moreover, we who by our prayers destroy all demons which stir up wars, violate oaths, and disturb the peace, are of more help to the emperors than those who seem to be doing the fighting . . . And though we do not become fellow-soldiers with him [the emperor], even if he presses for this, yet we are fighting for him and composing a special army of piety through our intercessions to God.'

'That was all very well when the Christians were only a minority group in the empire', commented Maureen shrewdly, 'but it was a different ball game when the emperors started Christianizing everything. There would have been no one left to fight any wars!'

'Which would have been absolutely wonderful!' contended Christobel in a militant tone.

'The barbarians would certainly have thought so', answered Maureen tartly. 'Although they were far from perfect, I'd rather have been ruled by a Roman emperor than raped and pillaged by Attila the Hun!'

An ominous rumble of thunder could be heard in the distance.

'Clearly Constantine's seizure of power brought about a major change in Christian attitudes to war and violence', concluded Wade. 'Before then Christian writers were pacifists. After it they sought to justify the fact that Christians were taking an active part in the government and defence of the State, which was an unforgivable betrayal of the ideals of Jesus and his first followers.'

'Matthew 10:34: "I did not come to bring peace but a sword . . ."' began Frank zealously.

'Perhaps we should now consider St Ambrose', intervened Derek hastily. 'What could you . . . er . . . find out about his attitude to war and violence?'

'Horrid little man', stated Christobel, her eyes flashing belligerently. 'When the emperor Gratian went off to fight the Goths (who were Arian Christians, therefore in Ambrose's eyes heretics) he went on as though Gratian was fulfilling the will of God.'

'But the imperial army ended up suffering a crushing defeat!' added Wade with a smirk.

'That did happen very early in his episcopacy', said Ruth in an excusing tone. 'I expect that he learnt from experience because he never again quite so exuberantly predicted victory. And, you know, he did stress the difference between just and unjust wars.

I'd read about that too, and was able to say that according to Ambrose a just war was one commanded by God or defensive in nature.

Derek gave me an encouraging smile, and Wade admitted that Ambrose wrote that treaties made with enemies should be honoured, no unfair advantage should be taken of them, and mercy should be granted to defeated foes.

Maureen then said that actually she thought that Ambrose had gone too far in loving his enemies. He had even condemned the use of violence in self-defence.

'But he believed that you were morally obliged to go to the assistance of someone else if they were being attacked, even if you could not help yourself', Wade pointed out.

'I think that's absolutely ridiculous', sniffed Christobel. 'All Violence Is Wrong!'

'Well, if I was being attacked and someone walked past and said sorry they couldn't help me because they were a Christian, I'd be bloody mad', said Maureen hotly.

'Do you think that Ambrose's background could have . . . er . . . influenced his attitude to war and violence?' asked Derek with a rather desperate look on his face.

'In *The Early Fathers on War and Violence* Swift mentions that Ambrose had a distinguished career as a Roman governor before he became a bishop', Wade replied, 'and hence it is not surprising that he was influenced by traditional Roman values: justice, courage, loyalty, public responsibility, and so on.'

'And he tried to fit them in with Christian values like love and forgiveness', said Ruth. 'He wrote that we should hate sin not sinners, and ultimately it is more important to pursue internal peace than defeat external enemies.'

'And he excommunicated the emperor Theodosius for having all those people at Thessalonica killed,' I managed to say, 'and he didn't go along with capital punishment or the clergy participating in war.'

Derek agreed, and mentioned that when Ambrose hadn't wanted to hand over a basilica to the Empress Justina he had offered only passive resistance.

'He refused to fight the imperial troops but organized a sort of non-violent sit-in', volunteered Maureen. 'He even got the congregation singing stirring hymns and psalms, which was the first time that was done in the western part of the empire. The more I think about it, the more Ambrose seems just the sort of person who'd chain himself to a railway line when a train carrying nuclear armaments was due to pass by. You would have got on real well with him, Christobel!'

Christobel acknowledged that if he'd protested against the manufacture and use of nuclear arms he would have gone some way toward atoning for his otherwise blatantly bigoted nature.

The heat was getting stifling and I was awfully glad when Derek said: 'What, then, can we . . . er . . . conclude about this topic?'

'I suspect that early Christians were just as ambivalent about war and military service as we are today', said Ruth with a twinkle in her eyes.

Before Christobel could get very far in denouncing weak-minded attitudes and asserting that, instead of being wimps, pacifists were really the most courageous people in society, the thunderstorm broke overhead.

'Superstitious people in the early Church would have taken this as a sign of divine intervention', remarked Wade.

'On the side of peace or . . . or . . . ?' stuttered Kirsty with a shiver.

'PACIFISM!' proclaimed Christobel.

'RIGHTEOUSNESS!' shouted Frank.

'Well, I just take it as a sign that the cool change is coming,' said Maureen bluntly, 'and thank God for that!'

# WEEK·ELEVEN

## Jesus Christ: God or godly?

It was Frank's turn to lead the group. He started off by declaring that the very first verse in the Bible reveals the Trinity of God because the Hebrew word for God (*Elohim*) is plural: 'In the beginning *Elohim* (plural) created the heavens and the earth . . .'

Wade leant back in his chair with his arms crossed and a sort of resigned I-knew-it-would-be-like-this expression on his face.

Frank ploughed steadily on through the Old Testament. Derek tried several times to speed him up, but Frank refused to be diverted from his chosen course. Twenty minutes went by and he hadn't even got to Isaiah.

'Yes, yes, we all had that preached to us when we were in our cradles', snapped Christobel at last. 'We're here today to discuss theological debates IN THE FOURTH CENTURY!'

'I'm coming to that', maintained Frank stubbornly. 'If you want a quick summary, God reveals in the Bible that there is the Trinity (Father, Son and Holy Spirit) and the bishops at the Council of Nicaea in AD 325 worked out the Nicene Creed:

We believe in one God, the Father, Almighty, Maker of all things visible and invisible:

And in one Lord Jesus Christ, the Son of God, begotten of the Father, Only-begotten, that is, from the substance of the Father; God from God, Light from Light, Very God from Very God, begotten not made, Consubstantial with the Father, by whom all things were made, both things in heaven and things in earth; who for us men and for our salvation came down and was incarnate, was made man, suffered, and rose again the third day, ascended into heaven, and is coming to judge living and dead.

And in the Holy Spirit.

And those who say "There was when he was not" and "Before his generation he was not", and "he came to be from nothing", or those who pretend that the Son of God is "Of other hypostasis or substance", or "created" or "alterable" or "mutable", the Catholic and Apostolic Church anathematizes.'

Frank slapped his folder shut with a satisfied air.

'Is that all you have to say, Frank?' Derek asked incredulously.

'I've got another twenty pages on the Trinity in the Bible, but Christobel here wanted to know what was going on in the fourth century, and that's it in a nutshell', replied Frank confidently.

Wade gave a derisive snort.

'It is extremely important,' he said to Frank, slowly and deliberately, like you speak to someone who's slightly deaf, 'that we look beyond the traditions and doctrines that Christians are so comfortable with to what was *really* going on in the early Church. Put aside your ingrained prejudices and you'll find that there is NO clear statement of the Trinity in the Hebrew Scriptures, in the Christian Scriptures, or in early Christian writings. In fact, writers before Constantine generally adopted a subordinationist position, if they considered the issue of Jesus' relationship to the Father at all.'

Kirsty, looking baffled, asked what a 'subordinationist position' was.

Derek then said that it might be helpful if we clarified some of the terms that were used in the early theological controversies.

'Subordinationists did not necessarily reject the divinity of Jesus, but they believed that he was subordinate to the Father', responded Wade in a condescending tone.

'Monarchianists stressed the oneness of God and his role as monarch of the universe', volunteered Christobel.

'But dynamic monarchianists, or adoptionists, thought that Jesus was a man who had been divinely energized by the Holy Spirit at his baptism', continued Wade. 'They are also sometimes called Paulianists after Paul of Samosata, who was bishop of Antioch from 260 to 272. Modalistic monarchianists, or modalists, on the other hand, argued that the three persons of the Trinity (Father, Son and Holy Spirit) were just three roles filled by the one God. Sabellius taught this *circa* 200, and hence modalists are sometimes known as Sabellians.'

Kirsty looked even more confused.

'What about Arius and . . . er . . . Alexander?' ventured Derek at last.

'Arius was a presbyter in Alexandria who came down heavily on the subordinationist side', expounded Wade knowledgeably. 'His teaching is probably best summed up in a poem or song he wrote, called the *Thalia*:

God was not always Father. There was a time when he was not yet Father; then he became Father. The Son was not always; for all things were made from the non-existent, and all existing creatures and works were made; so also the Word of God himself was made from the non-existent, and there was when he did not exist, and he was not before he was made, but he also had a beginning of creation. For God was alone, the word and wisdom did not yet exist . . .

By nature the Word is, like all of us, subject to change, but free in himself; he remains good as far as he wills . . .

The Word is not truly God. But if he is called God, nevertheless he is not truly; but by participation of grace . . . Just as all things are by nature alien to God and different from him, so too the Word is absolutely alien to the essence and property of the Father; he is of the order of works and creatures; he is one of them . . .'

'I must say that I don't think much of his writing skills', observed Maureen critically. 'What a boring song!'

'Alexander, bishop of Alexandria, didn't think much of his theology', responded Ruth with a smile. 'He convened a council of bishops which excommunicated Arius in 318.'

'But Arius had lots of friends and supporters who rallied to his defence!' pointed out Christobel.

'Thus creating a great controversy which irritated the emperor', added Wade. 'Constantine couldn't understand the theological issues involved (in fact, he described them as "small and very insignificant questions") but he was determined to preside over a united Church and empire.'

'And when negotiations between the parties broke down, he called the Council of Nicaea,' continued Christobel hotly, 'and after dazzling the assembled bishops with his wealth, power and generosity, he pressured them into agreeing to the Nicene Creed'.

'Which the Church has embraced ever since', commented Wade cynically. 'But, for all that, what difference would it really make to Christians if the doctrine of the Trinity was quietly done away with?'

'A lot of churches would have to change their names!' tittered Christobel.

'But Jesus is – really is – God . . . isn't he? I mean the Trinity really does exist, doesn't it?' stuttered Kirsty, a look of horror on her face. 'It's like . . . my Sunday School teacher used to say . . . $H_2O$ can be water or ice or steam . . . and that's sort of like Jesus and God and the Holy Spirit . . .'

'I personally believe that he was just a man', replied Wade coolly, 'but he was undoubtedly the greatest moral teacher who ever lived. If we all followed the Sermon on the Mount . . .'

'Oh, yes, he was just a man', interrupted Maureen in a sarcastic tone, 'who healed the sick, raised the dead, walked on water . . .'

'Well, of course, if you actually *believe* that the Bible is an accurate historical record . . .' responded Wade with a supercilious smile.

Frank, who had been getting angrier and angrier, lost the battle for self-control.

'All Scripture is inspired by God – it says so itself (2 Timothy 3:16). And what about people who are healed *today*, and rise from the dead *today*, and all other kinds of miracles that born-again Christians experience?' he bellowed, pointing his finger at Wade. 'If you had the faith of a little child that God wants you to have, perhaps you would experience them too!'

Wade said something about only believing in supernatural miracles if they were backed up by scientific proof, and if people did find healing at hyped-up Pentecostal rallies it was probably because most illnesses were psychosomatic anyway.

'Naturally, I can't accept that the Bible is an accurate

historical record', intervened Christobel before Frank could find adequate words to respond, 'but I'm convinced that mystical, supernaturalish things do happen. Jesus *could* have walked on water and healed people and that kind of thing. But as to whether he was man or God, I like the adoptionist approach: that the Spirit of God descended on Jesus the man at his baptism and left when he was on the cross. It's the only logical explanation, because it must be totally impossible for God to be really *born* and really *die*.'

'HE HAD TO DIE TO SAVE YOU FROM YOUR SINS!' thundered Frank.

'I think a lot of preachers overdo the sin-talk', said Maureen sharply, 'but I really like the idea that God loved us so much that he sent his Son to live and die like one of us.'

Wade seized on the word 'Son'.

'Just suppose, for argument's sake, that Jesus really was the divine Son or Word of God', he asserted. 'Arius did not deny that he was, but he saw clear evidence in the Bible that the Son or Word had to be subordinate to the Father. How can you reconcile John 14:28 ("If you loved me, you would be glad that I am going to the Father, for the Father is greater than I") with the Nicene Creed?'

Having delivered this challenge he sat back again and folded his arms.

'You accept it by faith!' stated Frank emphatically.

'Oh, God!' murmured Wade, raising a hand to his eyes.

'Well, I think it's frightfully important for us to consider this issue, because it's so absolutely fundamental to our religious beliefs', remarked Christobel with a reproving glance at Frank.

'A long time ago I read a parable – I think it was attributed to Buddha', said Ruth reflectively. 'It went something like this. A man who had been shot by a poisoned arrow was found by a doctor who had the ability to remove the arrow and save his life. However, the victim insisted on first talking on and on about the type of arrow it was, who had shot him, and where he had gone. As a result he died before the doctor could save him.'

We all looked blankly at her for a minute.

'Christians don't have anything to do with Buddha', declared Frank, 'because he must have been inspired by the devil, but it seems to me that so-called Christian theologians like Arius aren't much better. They think they're experts, but they don't know what they're talking about. Saving souls is the only thing that really matters.'

Wade raised his eyes to the ceiling and Christobel clenched her fists. With long red fingernails like hers that must have been painful.

'You don't think that it was a good thing that bishops were forced to clarify Christian beliefs at Nicaea?' asked Derek rather feebly.

'*Were* they clarified?' asked Wade in a tone of mock wonder. 'I thought that the crucial term that was used in defining the Son's relationship to the Father (*homoousios*) meant different things to different bishops. That was why they could all agree to it. And bitter controversies continued long after 325.'

Christobel absolutely agreed.

'Actually, a year or two after the Council of Nicaea, Constantine came to quite favour the Arian side', she observed. 'Arius himself had been sent into exile, but Constantine ordered him back. Athanasius was bishop of Alexandria by then, and he was frightfully nasty to poor Arius. He later said that Arius's sudden death the day before he was to be reinstated to his position of presbyter was due to divine providence, but, if you ask me, he was probably poisoned.'

'Athanasius was the most vocal defender of the Nicene Creed in the fourth century', went on Wade, 'and as a result he annoyed Constantine, and later Constantine's son Constantius, so much that he ended up being sent into exile five times. In fact, if pro-Nicene Theodosius hadn't beome emperor in 379 we might all be Arians today!'

'The Holy Spirit has made sure we know the truth', maintained Frank.

'Helped by the repressive measures adopted by the Roman State and the mainstream Church', added Wade savagely.

It was time to finish up. Christobel, Wade and Frank left straightaway, Frank muttering something about non-Christians and the devil as he marched out.

Kirsty remained seated, looking awfully pale and upset.

'I thought that I would really enjoy studying Church history', she said, blinking back tears, 'but all this course has done is fill me with doubts!'

Had never seen Ruth look so cross.

'It can be interesting and helpful to consider and discuss theological issues, but none of us can possibly gain a full understanding of the nature of God', she declared with unusual vigour. 'Kirsty, it is not a cop-out to say that the relationship between the Father and the Son and the Holy Spirit is a mystery which we cannot fully explain. That is part of the fascination of theology, for me at least. Words and concepts and analogies are never adequate. God is above them all.'

'I'm not a theologian', confided Derek, 'but it seems to me that a number of heresies have arisen simply because people have taken one aspect of God's nature and pushed it too far. Take Arius for example. He was so intent on safeguarding the . . . er . . . unique position of God the Father that inevitably this led him to . . . er . . . demote the position of the Son. And some people have placed so much stress on Jesus' divinity that they have ended up denying his humanity, and vice versa.'

'Well, I heard a really good sermon last Sunday', said Maureen bracingly. 'I almost didn't go to church because I was expecting my daughter and son-in-law to call in on their way home from their honeymoon and I wanted to be there when they opened their presents, but at 10.15 they rang to say that they couldn't make it until after lunch, so I was able to get to church just in time to hear the sermon. And it was all about Jesus being God. The preacher reckoned that while Jesus may not have come out and directly said that he was God, he did things that the Jews knew that only God could do, like forgiving sins. And John the Baptist said that he wasn't worthy enough to untie Jesus' sandals, which was another way of saying that he wasn't worthy of being Jesus' slave. And Jesus himself is supposed to have said that when two or three came together in his name he would be with them, which, according to my minister, was a paraphrase of a rabbinic saying: when two or three rabbis gathered together in judgement the glory of God would be in the midst of them. That's the kind of statement that would have made the religious leaders hate Jesus and want to kill him.'

Maureen paused for breath.

'And now that I come to think of it, why *did* they want to kill him if it wasn't because they thought that he was claiming to be God?' she asked enthusiastically. 'And what changed Peter and the other disciples from snivelling cowards into men brave enough to preach about Jesus, suffer persecution and die horrible deaths? It must have been something pretty dramatic – like Jesus rising from the dead!'

Kirsty began to look more cheerful, and we decided to go to the refectory for morning tea.

# WEEK·TWELVE

## More disputes

Really exhausted after presenting my first tutorial paper. It took me ages to work out what went on in the late fourth, early fifth centuries, but at last I think I have got it sorted out.

The fourth-century Arian controversy focused on Jesus' relationship to the Father. How could he be God? The Council of Nicaea decided that he was 'identical in essence' with the Father, 'God from God, Light from Light', etc.

This, however, did not stop theological disputes. Another question was raised. If Jesus was God, how do you explain the Bible's references to his human experiences? In other words, how could God be born a baby, 'grow in wisdom' (Luke 2:52), suffer thirst, weariness, pain, grief, and ultimately death? Among pro-Nicene, anti-Arian Christians two main responses to this thorny question developed, one associated more with Alexandria and the other with Antioch.

The Alexandrians tended to stress the divinity of Christ. The divine, eternal Word of God accommodated himself to the conditions of humanity.

An extreme version of this concept was put forward by Apollinarius (c.310-390). Actually, he was bishop of Laodicea, which is not far from Antioch, but he was a great friend of

Athanasius, bishop of Alexandria. He argued that the divine spirit of God took the place of a human mind in Jesus Christ.

The implication of this teaching was that Jesus' human experiences were little more than play-acting. Not surprisingly, Apollinarianism was condemned by a Roman council in 377, the Council of Constantinople in 381, and by the emperor Theodosius in an official edict in 388.

The Antiochenes, on the other hand, tended to stress the humanity of Jesus as well as his divinity. They could then attribute his human experiences to human nature.

Two of the most vocal Antiochene theologians were Diodore, bishop of Tarsus (died 390), and his disciple Theodore, bishop of Mopsuestia (died 428). They firmly believed that in Jesus there was a union of two distinct natures, human and divine. In response to Apollinarianism they stressed the reality of Jesus' humanity.

Pushed to its extreme, their teaching could imply that there were two Christs, one being only a man adopted by God and granted slightly more grace than the Old Testament prophets. Like Apollinarianism this version was condemned, although not until after Diodore's death.

Debates continued into the fifth century, and a showdown between rival christologies took place soon after Nestorius (a monk from Antioch) was made bishop of Constantinople in 428.

Nestorius became disturbed by popular devotion to Mary, and in particular by references to her as *Theotokos* (mother of God). At best he could only accept that she was *Christotokos* (mother of Christ). He scandalized many by saying that God could not be a baby two or three months old.

Enter Cyril, bishop of Alexandria from 412 to 444. He wrote three letters to Nestorius rebuking his teaching. To the last one he added twelve anathemas which, among other things, condemned anyone who denied Mary the title *Theotokos*, divided the words and acts of Christ between human and divine natures, and did not confess that the Word of God suffered in the flesh, was crucified in the flesh, and tasted death in the flesh.

This was a slap in the face not just to Nestorius but to Antiochene theology in general. Other theologians entered the fray, and a pamphlet war broke out between the rival parties.

The harassed emperor (Theodosius II) called a council of bishops to meet at Ephesus in June 431. When John, bishop of Antioch, and his supporters arrived four days late, they found that Cyril and his supporters had already condemned and deposed Nestorius. They then called a rival council which condemned Cyril, who in turn had them condemned by his council. Both sides appealed to the emperor to ratify their decisions—and he did, placing Nestorius, John *and* Cyril under arrest. Cyril managed to bribe his way back to Alexandria, while Nestorius expressed a weary wish to return to his monastery in Antioch, which was promptly granted.

After pressure from the emperor and much negotiation, a reconciliation was worked out between Cyril and John in 433. Neither was completely victorious. Cyril couldn't get his twelve anathemas accepted, and John had to agree to the term *Theotokos* and the deposition and exile of Nestorius. The formula that they agreed to was as follows:

> We confess, therefore, our Lord Jesus Christ, the only-begotten Son of God, perfect God and perfect Man, consisting of a rational soul and a body begotten of the Father before the ages as touching his Godhead, the same, in the last days, for us and for our salvation, born of the Virgin Mary, as touching his Manhood; the same of one substance with the

Father as touching his Godhead, and of one substance with us as touching his Manhood. For of two natures a union has been made. For this cause we confess one Christ, one Son, one Lord.

In accordance with this sense of the unconfused union, we confess the holy Virgin to be *Theotokos,* because God the Word became incarnate and was made man, and from the very conception united himself to the temple taken from her. And as to the expressions concerning the Lord in the Gospels and Epistles, we are aware that theologians understand some as common, as relating to one Person, and others they distinguish, as relating to two natures, explaining those that befit the divine nature according to the Godhead of Christ, and those of a humble sort according to his Manhood. (Stevenson, *Creeds, Councils and Controversies,* p 291 )

This was the basis of the definition approved by the Council of Chalcedon in 451.

When I'd finished reading my paper to the group, Derek thanked me for giving a good summary of a very complex and controversial period in history. He then asked whether we thought that Nestorius had been orthodox or not.

'I reckon he was right to tell people not to call Mary "mother of God"', declared Frank in an approving tone. 'It's downright sinful the way Catholics worship her as though she was a pagan goddess. And they make such a thing about her virginity! She was certainly a virgin when Jesus was born, but the Bible clearly says that she had lots of other children. Do Catholics think they were conceived by the Holy Ghost too? Ha-ha-ha!'

Felt really embarrassed, because Ruth was sitting right opposite me.

'It is interesting that devotion to Mary arose at a time

when pagan goddesses were going out of fashion, isn't it?' she responded blandly.

'It shows how important women really are', interjected Christobel. 'Most people can really relate only to a female deity. But to get back to Nestorius, I absolutely abhor terms like "orthodox" and "heretic". Everyone is entitled to their own particular viewpoint, and quarrels like the one between Nestorius and Cyril simply arise through prejudice and misunderstanding. Sadly, in the Nestorius-Cyril dispute misunderstanding was largely caused by the fact that there wasn't a suitable terminology to describe Christ's humanity and divinity. The Greek-speaking Eastern theologians didn't all mean the same thing by terms like *homoousios*, *hypostasis* and *prosopon*, while as for the Latin West . . .'

She made an airy gesture.

'Yes, but what we should really consider is the hidden agenda in the christological disputes', said Wade firmly. 'The theological issues merely masked power struggles between the bishops of the great Christian centres. Traditional rivalries were exacerbated in 381 when the Council of Constantinople resolved that "the bishop of Constantinople shall have rank after the bishop of Rome because it is the New Rome". This offended Rome, because it implied that Rome's claim to primacy was dependent on its former secular standing as capital of the empire, and it enraged Alexandria, which for a long time had laid claim to being the greatest Christian city in the East. Hence, bishops of Alexandria usually missed no opportunity to put down their counterparts in Constantinople, and they could generally count on Rome's support. They could also expect assistance from cities in Asia Minor, like Ephesus, which were hostile to Constantinople, and (in the Nestorian dispute) from Cyprus and Jerusalem, because they were hostile to Antioch.'

'Well, I didn't think much of Cyril of Alexandria', commented Maureen trenchantly. 'His enormous power and wealth must have gone to his head. He was implicated in anti-Semitic and anti-pagan riots and the murder of some woman . . .'

'Hypatia, a distinguished Neoplatonist philosopher', supplied Christobel, torn between pride in female achievement and virtuous indignation at her untimely death. 'However, Nestorius was little better. He was heavily into persecuting the poor Arian Christians, and was nicknamed Firebrand after an Arian church was destroyed.'

'What can we . . . er . . . conclude about the results of the controversies?' asked Derek in an uneasy tone.

'In 433 John of Antioch had to accept the deposition of Nestorius, but Cyril had to make considerable doctrinal concessions', responded Ruth quietly. 'And Nestorius believed that Pope Leo's doctrinal statement (the *Tome* which was presented to the Council of Chalcedon in 451) vindicated his position. However, the council reiterated his condemnation as a heretic, and approved as orthodox the "letters of Cyril to Nestorius", which some people thought included the twelve anathemas.'

Very confusing. Maureen said that the whole controversy had been a waste of time, because no one had been able to adequately explain how Jesus could be both man and God. In her opinion, people should just accept that it's a mystery and not try to perform spiritual autopsies.

'This topic does sort of raise the issue of Church government, doesn't it?' ventured Kirsty. 'How can disputes between church leaders and theologians sort of be resolved?'

'By everyone listening to the Holy Spirit!' replied Frank forcefully.

'By women participating equally in the decision-making

process!' cried Christobel. 'Only then will the Church truly reflect the body of Christ!'

'By the Church being truly democratic and taking into account the needs and opinions of the marginalized, regardless of age, sex, and race', amended Wade carefully.

'I'm all for democracy in theory,' remarked Maureen reflectively, 'but I can't stand committees. I got talked into joining the church property committee last year, and the amount of time I've wasted at meetings is unbelievable. It took two hours last week just to decide what colour to paint the back door of the hall.'

Derek kindly asked if there was anything that I would like to say to conclude the discussion. Couldn't think of anything, except to say that I think that I'm definitely not cut out to be a theologian or a bishop.

'The whole Church could do without them', muttered Frank.

'I wonder,' said Ruth musingly, 'whether the result would be anarchy – or heaven!'

# WEEK·THIRTEEN

## A great preacher

Wade's turn to lead the tutorial. He announced in a very businesslike way that he had divided the topic into four sections: Who was John Chrysostom? Why did he preach about social issues? What was the result? and, Why did this happen? He planned to discuss the first three and we could contribute our thoughts to the fourth.

Who was Chrysostom? Wade said that he was born in Antioch sometime between 344 and 354. His father died while he was very young and he was brought up by his mother (that gave Christobel an opportunity to point out the importance of women). In his late teens he became a fervent Christian and spent a number of years living as a hermit in the Syrian desert. He was ordained a priest by the bishop of Antioch in 386 and appointed to preach in the principal church of the city. He became so famous as a preacher that after his death he was named Chrysostom, which means 'golden-mouthed'.

Why had he preached about social issues? Antioch, according to Wade, was one of the largest cities in the Roman Empire in Chrysostom's time. Some of its quarter-of-a-million inhabitants enjoyed fabulous wealth but many lived in appalling poverty. Beggars resorted to all kinds of measures to attract alms, such as chewing old shoes, driving nails into their heads, and even mutilating their children.

Wade read one of John's sermons, as John would have thundered from his pulpit to his well-to-do audience:

The poor man whom you have defrauded is suffering anguish
    because of the lack of the necessities of life . . .
He may go about the market-place in the evening,
    not knowing where he is to spend the night.
How can the unhappy fellow sleep,
    with pangs in the belly,
        tortured by hunger,
            while it is freezing and the rain coming down
                on him?
And while you are coming home from the bath,
    clean and dandy,
        dressed in soft clothes,
            full of contentment and happiness,
            and hastening to sit down to
                splendidly prepared dinners,
he is driven everywhere about the market-place
    by cold and hunger,
        with his head hung low and his hands outstretched.
The poor man does not even have the courage to ask for the
    necessary food
        from one so well fed
        and so well rested,
            and often has to withdraw
                covered with insults.
When, therefore, you have returned home,
    when you lie down on your couch,
        when the lights around your house shine bright,
            when your table is well prepared and plentiful,
at that time remember
    the poor miserable man
        wandering about like a dog in the alleys,

in darkness and in mire . . .
And you would throw the whole house in confusion,
    if you but see a drop of water falling from the ceiling,
        calling for the slaves and disturbing everything,
        while he,
            laid in rags,
                and straw,
                    and dirt,
                        has to bear the bitter cold . . .

Kirsty shivered and Christobel wiped a tear from her eyes with a lace handkerchief.

'And what was the result of Chrysostom's preaching?' asked Wade briskly. 'His fame as an orator spread to the imperial court and he was made bishop of Constantinople against his will in 398. He strove to reform the moral and spiritual life of the city, but within ten years he had been deposed and had died in exile. WHY DID THIS HAPPEN?'

Wade sat back in his chair and folded his arms.

'Well, he seems to have been a good, upright Christian, so he would have been opposed by the devil', said Frank.

Wade accorded him a disdainful glance.

'It gets back to what we talked about last week', claimed Christobel regretfully, 'all that absolutely horrid rivalry between Alexandria and Constantinople. Theophilus, bishop of Alexandria, was absolutely livid when he was summoned to Constantinople to appear before a special synod presided over by John to answer charges that he had mistreated some Egyptian monks, and he was utterly determined to stir up hatred toward John wherever he went. Finally he managed to get together another synod of thirty-six bishops (called the Synod of the Oak after the villa where they met), which declared poor John deposed.'

'But he wouldn't have succeeded in getting rid of him if

John hadn't alienated the empress', argued Maureen. 'All his attacks on women wasting money on "extravagance, personal adornment and every other mark of the harlot" didn't go down too well in that quarter!'

'He was frightfully intolerant in that respect', agreed Christobel, idly fingering a long gold chain around her neck. 'Quite unreasonable!'

'The apostle Paul did say: "I want women to dress modestly, with decency and propriety, not with braided hair or gold or pearls or expensive clothes . . ."' pointed out Frank.

If looks could kill, Frank would have been writhing on the floor.

I managed to say that I thought that John could have offended well-to-do men as well as women by insisting that they share their wealth with the poor.

Wade nodded approvingly and launched into preaching mode, quoting from another one of John's many extant sermons.

Tell me, then, where do you get your riches from?
From whom did you receive it . . .?
  'From my father and he from my grandfather.'
But can you, going back through many generations, show that the riches were justly acquired?
No, you cannot. The root and origin of them must have been injustice.
Why?
Because God in the beginning made not one man rich and another poor . . . Rather, he left the earth free to all alike . . .
Is not 'the earth God's, and the fullness thereof'? If then our possessions belong to one common Lord, they belong also to our fellow-servants. The possessions of the Lord are all common
. . .

'He sounds like a communist!' interrupted Maureen incredulously. 'I'm all for charity, but that's taking things too far.'

'He continually exhorted people to give alms to the poor,' remarked Ruth mildly, 'but he didn't, to my knowledge, advocate an economic system that did away with private property altogether.'

'He wasn't exactly a communist in the modern sense of the word', conceded Wade, 'but he strongly denounced economic and social inequality and the exploitation of the poor by the ruling classes. "Whence comes the great inequality of conditions in life? From the greed and arrogance of the rich. But, brethren, let us do away with this situation . . ."'

'Can you think of any other reasons why he might have been . . . er . . . unpopular in Constantinople?' asked Derek.

'Unfortunately, not all of the clergy in Constantinople welcomed his quest to correct abuses and impose rigorous moral standards . . .' began Ruth.

'Conflict would naturally develop between two very different Christian lifestyles,' interposed Wade coolly, 'the rigorous asceticism of the Syrian monks and the comfortable, cosmopolitan life of the "establishment" clergy in Constantinople.'

'I read that he sort of thought that Christian perfection should be the aim of all believers, not just the clergy', ventured Kirsty.

'Yes', corroborated Ruth with an encouraging smile. 'Frances Young concludes in her book *From Nicaea to Chalcedon* (p 159) that "Christianity is not simply a set of disputed doctrines, but a way of life, and Chrysostom never lets this be forgotten." I thought that was interesting in view of the theological disputes we have been considering in the last couple of weeks.'

'But it's so awfully difficult to be a perfect Christian', said Kirsty with a sigh.

'It is certainly difficult to be true to the values espoused by Jesus and live in secular Western society', affirmed Wade condescendingly. 'However, it is not impossible. If we learn from developments in liberation theology and accept that the struggle for social justice should be an integral part of the Christian life. . .'

'From what I've heard, that liberation theology stuff is downright demonic', broke in Frank. 'God says in 1 Peter that everyone should submit to the ruling authorities and slaves should obey their masters, and if we have to suffer for being a Christian we should then rejoice because we are participating in the sufferings of Christ . . .'

'Yes, yes, we went through all that weeks ago when we talked about persecution', snapped Christobel. 'To get back to John Chrysostom and why he was deposed and exiled, it's frightfully obvious that he was the wrong person for the job. It was one thing to preach absolutely brilliant socialist sermons in a provincial city, but they were quite unsuitable in the imperial capital where everything (unfortunately) depended on the good will of the emperor and empress. So tactless! A woman would have done a much better job.'

'Well, I think he was mad', stated Maureen forcefully.

We all looked at her in surprise.

'It says in the book I read that before he became a priest he went to live on his own in a cave in the Syrian mountains, tried not to sleep, and didn't lie down at all for TWO WHOLE YEARS! If that isn't madness, what is? And,' pursued Maureen doggedly, when no one answered, 'as a result of his not lying down he ended up with gastric and kidney problems, which doubtless made his temper worse and contributed to his lack of popularity. My ex-husband was hell to live with when he had his stomach ulcer.'

Wasn't quite sure of the medical or historical value of this, but Derek said rather feebly that it was an interesting point to consider.

'Er . . . next week we will look at the ascetic movement in greater detail. Is there anything further that you would like to . . . er . . . say, Wade?'

'Merely that John Chrysostom is rightly regarded as one of the most outstanding Christian preachers who ever lived', responded Wade majestically, 'and his deposition was a great tragedy. An even greater tragedy, however, is the collaboration between Christianity and capitalism that is entrenched in Western culture.'

'And the collaboration between so-called Christians and communist insurrectionists', grumbled Frank, but fortunately Wade was too busy telling Christobel about a brilliant new liberation theology book he'd just discovered to take any notice.

# WEEK·FOURTEEN

## The development of monasticism

Derek introduced today's topic. From the beginning of the Christian Church there have been men and women who have chosen to live a celibate and ascetic lifestyle, but the monastic movement really took off in the third and fourth centuries. St Antony, who lived from 251 to 356 (105 years!), was one of the most famous and influential early ascetics. Derek hoped that we had all read about him. What had we been able to find?

'He was the son of fairly well-to-do Egyptian peasants', commented Maureen, 'and about six months after they died he heard a passage from Matthew 19 read in church: "If you would be perfect, go, sell what you possess and give to the poor, and you will have treasure in heaven." He took that literally, whacked his poor little sister into a convent, and rushed off to be a hermit. A bit impetuous, if you ask me.'

'He had the most amazing spiritual experiences', exclaimed Kirsty. 'He actually spent years locked up IN A TOMB, and the devil tried all kinds of things to break his faith and commitment. This is what his biographer wrote (she picked up a copy of Athanasius's *The Life of Antony*):

The place [that is the tomb] was . . . filled with the appearance of lions, bears, leopards, bulls, and serpents, asps, scorpions and wolves, and each of these moved in accordance with its form. The lion roared, wanting to spring at him; the bull seemed intent on goring; the creeping snake did not quite reach him; the onrushing wolf made straight for him— and altogether the sounds of all the creatures that appeared were terrible, and their ragings were fierce. Struck and wounded by them, Antony's body was subject to yet more pain . . .

'But he continued to maintain his faith in the Lord, and eventually

he saw the roof being opened, as it seemed, and a certain beam of light descending toward him. Suddenly the demons vanished from view, the pain of his body ceased instantly, and the building was once more intact . . . Antony entreated the vision that appeared, saying, "Where were you? Why didn't you appear in the beginning, so that you could stop my distress?" And a voice came to him: "I was here, Antony, but I waited to watch your struggle. And now, since you persevered and were not defeated, I will be your helper forever, and I will make you famous everywhere." '

'Anyone locked in a tomb for years with hardly any food and water would naturally get hallucinations', scoffed Wade.

Kirsty looked deflated, but protested that lots and lots of people thought that Antony was a really holy man and tried to imitate his hermit lifestyle. That created quite a problem for him when he came out from the tomb, because he had to keep going further and further into the desert to escape from his would-be disciples!

Wade could explain Antony's popularity too.

'Some of his followers would have been committed Christians who fled to the desert in protest against the replacement of Jesus' values by those of Constantine in the fourth-century Church', he reluctantly conceded. 'However, many were probably trying to escape unemployment, heavy taxation and conscription into the Roman imperial army.'

'Devoting yourself to chastity, endless prayer and starving was, of course, an easy way out!' observed Maureen sarcastically.

'Whatever reason they had for becoming hermits, it certainly wasn't scriptural', put in Frank aggressively. 'Christians are called to go into the world to win people for Christ, not run off into the desert . . .'

'I found Athanasius's story of Antony absolutely fascinating,' intervened Christobel, 'but it can hardly be described as good history. The underlying theme is really Athanasius's frightful prejudice against the poor Arians.'

'What about other forms of monastic life?' asked Derek.

'Pachomius, another Egyptian, who lived from 286 to 346, felt called to organize a community of monks', responded Ruth. 'The monks committed themselves to a life of humility and obedience to a superior, as well as to chastity and poverty.'

'Which is downright unscriptural', butted in Frank again. 'Paul said in Galatians that "it is for freedom that Christ has set us free. Stand firm, then, and do not let yourselves be burdened again by the yoke of slavery." But that's just what those monks did. They were like the Pharisees with their rules and regulations. They were trying to earn their salvation instead of just accepting it by faith. And they called their superior "abba" or "father", which directly breaks Jesus' command to "not call anyone on earth 'father', for you have one Father, and he is in heaven" (Matthew 23:9).'

Wade looked at him coldly.

'I find it significant,' he said in a haughty tone, 'that

although the first monks were theoretically attempting to withdraw from the world, they very soon established quite prosperous agricultural communities, engaged in trade, and often entertained visitors . . .'

'At least that's relatively normal', interrupted Maureen. 'Some really bizarre things went on in Syria. Some hermits ran around naked, others tied heavy iron chains to their legs, and Simeon Stylites sat on top of a fifty-foot column for forty years!'

'Never coming down?' asked Christobel incredulously. 'How did he . . . you know . . . attend to personal hygiene?'

'He didn't', replied Maureen bluntly. 'If you were an ascetic, you disregarded the corrupt old body and concentrated on Saving The Soul.'

'Athanasius says that Antony never washed at all, and he wore the same hair shirt and sheepskin for years and years', volunteered Kirsty helpfully.

Christobel gave a fastidious shudder.

'How absolutely horrid. His fingernails! His hair! He could have had lice!'

'Perhaps it was a good thing that Simeon stayed up his pole, after all', reflected Maureen. 'He wouldn't have stunk so much in the open air.'

'But it wasn't biblical', stated Frank adamantly. 'Who ever heard of Jesus sitting on a pole?'

'The ascetics thought that they were engaged in spiritual warfare, combating the devil', observed Ruth in her gentle way.

'And, incredible though it seems, they were often highly respected as Christian leaders', added Wade. 'Through conquering the temptations of the flesh they were thought to have gained greater access to God than ordinary mortals. They could thus mediate between God and humanity, perform miracles, and protect society from demonic forces. Furthermore, as they had deliberately rejected normal, everyday life, they were thought to be in a position to give impartial advice and mediate in disputes of a secular nature. For example, if two people in a village were fighting over who owned a piece of land, they would submit their case to the local hermit for judgment.'

'Yes', agreed Maureen vigorously. 'Simeon apparently sat on his pole healing, prophesying, going through lawsuits, and giving advice to the government. His approval was even required for the Council of Ephesus in 431 and the Council of Chalcedon in 451!'

'It still wasn't biblical!' maintained Frank stubbornly.

'Did you read anything about other forms of monastic life?' asked Derek rather desperately.

'Basil of Caesarea, who lived between 330 and 379, probably would have agreed with you, Frank, that wild eccentricities weren't quite in keeping with our Lord's teaching and the example of his life', said Ruth with a smile. 'He firmly believed that Christians should love and serve their neighbours, and when he started a monastic community on his family estate, he attached to the monastery a hospital, orphanage and workshop for the unemployed.'

Frank was temporarily silenced.

'That's frightfully good, of course,' acknowledged Christobel, 'but the foundation of true monastic life must be spiritual. I was absolutely fascinated by Evagrius of Pontus and John Cassian and their wonderful mystical theology . . .'

'Then along came St Benedict and his rule,' concluded Maureen quickly, 'which apparently dominated Western monasticism in the Middle Ages. And I must admit that although I wouldn't like to be a monk, the rule does seem quite moderate in comparison with the antics of Antony and Simeon and co.'

'But it's not biblical', reiterated Frank through clenched teeth.

'How often have you walked on water lately?' asked Wade rudely. 'That's biblical, isn't it?'

'Er . . . the point I wanted to make was that the monastic movement was not a simple, uniform phenomenon', rushed in Derek. 'And Peter Brown traces different effects of the movement in the eastern and western parts of the Roman Empire (in *The World of Late Antiquity*, p 110). Er . . . in the West

> the monastery became a means of sharpening the self-consciousness of the Catholic Church. The monastic establishment provided the bishop with the first truly professional clergy . . . The men who grew up in a bishop's monastery . . . were cut off from their fellows by vows of chastity and poverty, and by distinctive dress; and, being often educated only on the Holy Scriptures, they no longer shared in a classical education. They had become a professional élite, with their own solidarities, their own jargon, and an acute sense of superiority over "the world".

'However,

> In the East, by contrast, monasticism did not stand aloof. It flowed directly into the life of the great cities . . . the monks, with their new popularity, were the midwives of the process by which Christianity – in the late third century a minority-group dangerously limited to the towns—became the religion of the masses of the eastern empire. The growth of the monks had underpinned the narrow structure of the Christian Church. The monasteries harnessed the chronic underemployment of the towns and villages to service in the

Christian Church; by 418, the patriach of Alexandria could count on over 600 zealous monastic retainers. The labour of the monks in hospitals, in food-supply centres, in burial associations brought the presence of the Church home to the average townsman. In Upper Egypt, the monks who had terrorized the pagans also organized an ambulance service, carrying and nursing the wounded during a barbarian invasion . . .'

'I can just see you as an Eastern monk, Frank,' said Maureen encouragingly, 'rushing around terrorizing pagans. And Wade, you would have made a really good professional clergyman in the West.'

'I would have been a mystic,' cried Christobel excitedly, 'and Derek would have been a scholar. But what about the rest of you?'

'I wouldn't have minded being a member of a convent which ran an orphanage', confided Ruth.

'I know being a nun is awfully noble, but I don't really think I would have liked to have been one', said Kirsty worriedly.

'Well, I'm sure that I would have been hard put to have kept a vow of obedience for one week,' concluded Maureen honestly, 'let alone a lifetime, so I'd better not have been a nun either. But if nobody in the Middle Ages had been prepared to sacrifice themselves on the altar of marriage and family responsibility, where would the world be today?'

Where indeed?

Had to admit that I also suspect that I wouldn't have wanted to have been a monk, of the Eastern or Western variety, but I can't help but admire the men and women who had the faith, commitment and courage to take up those forms of Christian life.

Asked Neville on the way out what he would have liked to

have been. He said a Franciscan friar because he liked animals. Christobel intervened and said that St Francis of Assisi hadn't started his order until the thirteenth century, and what would Neville have done before then?

Neville mumbled something about probably being just a peasant, whereupon Christobel gave him a stern lecture on the value of positive thinking, and insisted that he attend a workshop that a friend of hers was going to conduct on Being True to Oneself.

'On second thoughts, I think I would have been an ascetic like Antony', he savagely whispered to me as we walked away. 'There are a lot worse things in life than being alone with God in the countryside!' ???

# WEEK·FIFTEEN

## Confessions

At last our final tutorial! We finished the course by reading
*The Confessions* of St Augustine. *The Confessions* is a sort of
autobiography written to God, and describes Augustine's
early life and conversion to Christianity in 386. The actual
tutorial topic was a bit strange, I thought: To what extent
does reading St Augustine's *Confessions* sum up your
experience of studying Church history?

Pondered over this for a while. I found the first chapters of
the book pretty heavy going and can't say that I really
enjoyed reading them, but I gradually began to get
interested in Augustine and ended up quite liking his book.
Realized that my experience of studying Church history was
very similar. I initially wondered what on earth had hit me,
but ended up very interested in it. Confessed this to the
group when we met. Kirsty admitted that she felt the same
way.

Christobel was more struck by Augustine's search for
truth.

'Isn't it absolutely fascinatingly significant that deep down
we are all Searching For Truth, for Meaning To Existence,
for an Understanding Of The Spiritual World? And, like so
many of the wonderful characters we have come across in
early Church history, Augustine was attracted to philosophy

and to a marvellously unorthodox, quasi-Christian religion, Manicheism. He also confronted issues we have considered, like how could a good God create a world full of evil, and how could Christ be divine and yet come to earth as a man. And he was influenced by St Ambrose whom we studied, and above all by his mother, Monica, which really goes to show that women played a very significant role in the early Church, even if it was a sadly undervalued one. But I can't help but feel that Monica went too far with Augustine, forever crying and praying for him and chasing him all over the Mediterranean. If a psychoanalyst was to analyse their relationship . . .'

'If you were a mother you'd know that you can't help but want the best for your children', snapped Maureen heatedly. 'You devote the best years of your life to wiping their dirty bottoms, and cooking and cleaning and ironing. If I had a pound for every shirt of my ex-husband's I ironed I'd be a millionaire, not to mention those hundreds of pages of Golf Club minutes I typed, or all those firm dinners I catered for . . .'

To our great surprise and dismay she burst into tears. We all sat stunned. Christobel was frozen with her mouth open and one arm in the air.

'I'm sorry, I'm sorry', sobbed Maureen uncontrollably. 'My divorce was finalized yesterday and everything suddenly got too much for me. I have to start looking for a job and my lovely house has got to be sold and I'll probably end up in some horrid little flat without a garden . . .'

'Oh, you poor darling!' cried Christobel, throwing her arms around Maureen. 'I know as a Christian I'm supposed to love and forgive everyone, but honestly, men can be such PIGS! Now, Maureen, I'm not going to let you catch the bus home; I'll drive you to my place for a cup of tea, and I'll introduce you to a friend of mine who runs an absolutely wonderful Christian support group for women from broken marriages; and I have another friend who's going overseas for a couple of years and wants someone to live in her townhouse, and it's truly lovely with a delightful courtyard garden, and she doesn't want much rent, just someone who'll take good care of her things and feed the garden and water the cat, and I know you'll absolutely love it, and we were only praying last night that the right tenant would come along . . .'

Maureen blew her nose, with a hanky thoughtfully supplied by Ruth, and tearfully thanked Christobel and the rest of us for being such a help to her. Felt really undeserving of such appreciation, but Maureen went on to say that she didn't know how she would have survived the last five months without the Early Church History course to take her mind off her marriage break-up. Whenever she hadn't been able to sleep at night she'd done her tutorial reading.

Kirsty echoed Maureen's thanks.

'Coming to live in the city and starting university was a lot harder than I thought it would be', she confided. 'And I've often felt sort of homesick and lonely, but you've always been so friendly, even when I've been really dumb and not understood what you've been talking about.'

It may have been just the way she was sitting, but she was looking particularly at Ruth, Derek and me. As with Maureen, I felt conscious of how little I'd really done to help her.

Had a sudden thought. Perhaps I could ask her to go to see a movie with me when the exams are over.

'There's something I'd, I'd like to say too', stuttered Neville suddenly.

Realized with a shock that it was the first time that Neville had voluntarily spoken to the group as a whole during the entire fifteen weeks that we had been meeting.

'I've, I've really enjoyed this course. Found it really thought provoking. But, well, Augustine was an expert at public speaking. Had a job as a teacher of rhetoric. Not my thing. Public speaking, I mean. I did all the reading for the tutes, but when it came time to say something my mind went blank, someone else said what I wanted to say, or I just didn't have the courage to speak up.'

He flushed, and hung his head.

Had another thought. I could ask Neville to come to see the movie too.

I was trying to remember what films were being shown at the moment, when I became aware that Derek was confessing that as an undergraduate he had been too shy to speak in tutorials too, and so he could really identify with Neville. He hoped that now that Neville had taken the plunge and admitted his problem it would be easier for him to contribute to discussions next year.

'But perhaps we had better now . . . er . . . return to this week's topic', he concluded hastily, looking at his watch. 'Did anyone else find that reading St Augustine's *Confessions* somehow summed up their experience of studying church history?'

Dead silence.

Eventually Frank spoke up. He seemed a little less self-assured than usual.

'I guess what struck me most in both the book and the course was the greatness of God and the sinfulness of man', he commented quietly. 'I suppose you all realize that I'm what you might call a fundamentalist?'

We nodded.

'And I know that fundamentalists aren't too popular around here', he continued sadly.

He paused and seemed to stare blindly ahead.

'Reading *The Confessions* reminded me of all my sins. The worst Augustine seemed to do was steal a few pears from an orchard but I . . . oh, well, to cut a long story short, I stuffed up my life, first with alcohol, then drugs as well. Had to steal to get money—vicious circle. If those Pentecostal Christians hadn't visited me in jail I'd probably be dead by now.'

He brushed away a tear.

'Can't explain what becoming a born-again Christian meant to me, how it changed my life. There were still tough times when I got out of jail, but I just clung to God's promises in the Bible. That's why I get so upset when I hear people criticizing God's word, picking it to pieces. It means so much to me. And now I've got my wife and two little kids', he finished hoarsely. 'God has been so good.'

'It can often be difficult for Christians to . . . er . . . balance faith and serious scholarship', said Derek gently. 'Particularly when it comes to the Bible. I greatly respect your faith, Frank, but I'm glad to see that you are no longer . . . er . . . confining your reading solely to the Bible. We all face the danger of becoming rather narrow-minded and fixed in our beliefs, and perhaps missing something of the greatness of God as a result. There are many inspiring books available today that I am sure would . . . er . . . deepen your understanding of God and the Christian faith . . .'

'Oh, yes', agreed Frank, more exuberantly. 'I've just finished reading Dennis Bennett's *Nine O'Clock in the Morning*, about baptism in the Holy Spirit, and John Wimber's *Power Healing* and *Power Evangelism* . . .'

Couldn't resist glancing at Wade to see how he was taking this. He seemed different, somehow. Not his usual aggressive, disdainful self. More relaxed, reflective.

As if he could read my thoughts, Derek turned to Wade

and asked him what he thought of Augustine's *Confessions*.

Wade hesitated.

'A week ago I probably wouldn't have been too impressed by Augustine', he said slowly. 'Particularly by his conversion experience. You know the bit, when he was out in the garden, tormented by his desires and unable to commit himself to God, he heard what sounded like a child's voice say "take it and read" over and over again. Eventually he realized that it was a divine command and he opened up the Bible. He immediately saw a passage that was pertinent to his situation, and "it was as though the light of confidence flooded into . . . [his] heart and all the darkness of doubt was dispelled . . ."'

Wade hesitated again.

'A week ago I probably would have said that it must have been just a coincidence that he heard a child's voice and opened up to that particular passage, but, well . . .'

He gave a short laugh.

'Since then I've had a similar experience!'

That was a confession indeed! You could have knocked me over with a feather!

'Last Saturday I was alone in the house, very depressed. I'd just had another row with my wife, God seemed to be a million miles away, and I was wondering why on earth I was wasting my time training to be a Christian minister. But there was nothing else I could think of to do with my life. I was pretty well at the end of my tether, and as a last resort cried out: "O God, what should I do?" Then I heard—I swear I heard—a voice say: "Matthew 22:37 and 39". I looked it up (I don't mind admitting that my hands were trembling!) and there were the commandments: "Love the Lord your God with all your heart and with all your soul and with all your mind"; and "Love your neighbour as yourself". I realized that above all I lacked love. I didn't love God (he seemed too remote to be known, let alone loved) and I no longer really loved anyone else, not even my wife. I was all dried up inside, just fulfilling my family, church and social responsibilities through a strong sense of duty. But how can you manufacture love? I went down on my knees and said I was sorry to God and would he please help me. Then I got a strong feeling (not an audible voice this time but a really strong feeling) that I should turn to Psalm 100. I started reading it, forcing myself to praise God, to sing songs of praise. It was difficult at first, but I kept going and it gradually got easier. I actually began to *feel* like praising him.'

Wade gave a slightly embarrassed smile.

'I don't know exactly how long I went on like that, but after quite some time of praying and praising, my tongue sort of tripped up and the words continued to come out but not in English. It was so beautiful that I kept going. I'd never felt such peace before, "the peace that passeth understanding . . ."'

'Praise the Lord! Brother, you've been baptized in the Holy Spirit!' cried Frank jubilantly, slapping Wade on the back.

'And you can still speak in that . . . that other language?' said Chrisobel in a hushed voice, leaning forward with her eyes fixed intently on Wade's face.

Wade nodded bashfully.

'I can control it (speak louder, quicker, softer, etc.) but I certainly didn't invent it.'

'And you still feel sort of peaceful?' asked Kirsty, her eyes as round as saucers.

Wade laughed.

'I can't say that everything has gone wonderfully right ever since, but even when I missed my bus yesterday morning I didn't get uptight. And my wife and I are getting on much better now.'

'God certainly works in a mysterious way his wonders to perform', said Ruth with a beaming smile. 'Thank you for sharing that testimony, Wade. It was a lovely way to end our semester together.'

'Yes', agreed Derek happily. 'But before you go I must hand back your essays . . .'

'Not such a lovely way to end the semester!' we chorused.

But when Derek handed me back my essay I discovered that I had got an A. FANTASTIC !!!

We all decided to go to the university coffee shop when the tutorial finished. It was great to see how everyone took the trouble to draw Neville into the conversation. And who would have thought a week ago that Frank and Wade could sit together excitedly talking about the Holy Spirit?

Inevitably, there was some discussion about essay results. It turned out that Frank got a C-, Maureen a C, Kirsty a C+, Wade and Christobel both Bs, Ruth a B+, and me, of course, an A. Neville turned bright red and tried to avoid disclosing his grade. Had an awful thought, and I'm sure the rest did too. Perhaps poor Neville had failed. Derek, however, encouraged him to reveal all. Good old Neville had got an A + + !!!

# Suggested Further Reading

## Translations of primary sources

**Ancient Christian Writers.** Ed J Quasten and J C Plumpe. Westminster, Maryland and New York: Newman Press; London: Longmans Green, 1946–75.

**Ante-Nicene Christian Library.** Ed A Roberts and J Donaldson. Edinburgh: T & T Clark, 1867–72. American Edition: *Ante-Nicene Fathers*. New York: 1926.

**Library of Christian Classics.** Ed J Baillie, J T McNeil and H P van Dusen. Philadelphia: Westminster; London: SCM, 1953–69.

## Collections of primary sources

Bettenson, H ed. *The Early Christian Fathers*. Oxford, London and New York: Oxford University Press, 1969.

Bettenson, H ed. *The Later Christian Fathers*. London, New York and Toronto: Oxford University Press, 1970.

Eusebius of Caesarea. *The History of the Church From Christ to Constantine.* Translated by G Williamson. Harmondsworth, Middlesex: Pelican, 1965; New York: 1966.

Jurgens, W A ed. *The Faith of the Early Fathers*. 3 vols. Collegeville, Minnesota: Liturgical Press, 1970, 1979.

Petry, R C ed. A *History of Christianity: Readings in the History of the Church*, Vol 1. Grand Rapids: Baker, 1981.

Staniforth, M and A Louth eds. *Early Christian Writings*. Revised edition. Harmondsworth, Middlesex: Penguin, 1987.

Stevenson, J ed. *A New Eusebius: Documents Illustrating the History of the Church to AD 337.* Revised with additional documents by W H C Frend. London: SPCK, 1987.

Stevenson, J ed. *Creeds, Councils and Controversies: Documents Illustrative of the History of the Church AD 337–461.* Revised with additional documents by W H C Frend. London: SPCK, 1989.

## General surveys

Brown, P. *The World of Late Antiquity.* London: Thames & Hudson, 1971; New York: Harcourt Brace Jovanovich, 1971.

Chadwick, H. *The Early Church.* Harmondsworth, Middlesex: Penguin, 1967; Grand Rapids: Eerdmans, 1969.

Comby, J. *How to Read Church History,* Vol 1: *From the Beginnings to the Fifteenth Century.* Translated by J Bowden and M Lydamore. London: SCM, 1985; New York: Crossroad, 1989.

Danielou, J and H Marrou. *The Christian Centuries,* Vol 1: *The First Six Hundred Years.* London: Darton, Longman & Todd, 1964; New York: McGraw-Hill, 1964.

Dowley, T et al. *The History of Christianity.* A Lion Handbook. Berkhamsted, Herts: Lion Publishing, 1977.

Frend W H C. *The Early Church.* London: Hodder & Stoughton, 1965; Philadelphia: Fortress, 1982; London: SCM, 1982.

Frend, W H C. *The Rise of Christianity.* Philadelphia: Fortress Press, 1984; London: Darton, Longman & Todd, 1984.

Frend, W H C. *Saints and Sinners in the Early Church: Differing and Conflicting Traditions in the First Six Centuries.* London: Darton, Longman & Todd, 1985; Wilmington, Delaware: Michael Glazier, Theology and Life Series 11, 1985.

Gonzalez, J L. *A History of Christian Thought,* Vol 1: *From the Beginnings to the Council of Chalcedon in 451.* Nashville, Tennessee: Abingdon Press, 1970.

Hazlett, I ed. *Early Christianity: Origins and Evolution to AD 600.* London: SPCK, 1991.

Jedin, H and J P Dolan, eds. *A History of the Church.* 2 vols. New

York: Crossroad, 1980; London: Burns & Oates, 1980–1.

Kelly, J N. *Early Christian Doctrines*. 5th revised edition. London: A. & C. Black, 1977; New York: Harper & Row, 1978.

Quasten, J. *Patrology*. Vols 1 and 2. Westminster, Maryland: Newman Press, 1950, 1953.

von Campenhausen, H. *Ecclesiastical Authority and Spiritual Power*. Translated by J Baker. London: A. & C. Black, 1969.

Young, F. *From Nicaea to Chalcedon: A Guide to the Literature and its Background*. London: SCM, 1983; Philadelphia: Fortress, 1983.

## And in particular . . .

### WEEK ONE *Why study church history anyway?*

Carr, E H. *What is History?* Harmondsworth, Middlesex: Penguin, 1964.

Kelly, J. 'Why Study Early Church History?' in Hazlett, ed. *Early Christianity* (see above), pp 3–13.

McIntire, C T ed. *God, History and Historians: Modern Christian Views of History*. New York: Oxford University Press, 1977.

McIntire, C T and R A Wells eds. *History and Historical Understanding*. Grand Rapids: Eerdmans, 1984.

### WEEK TWO *What were the Christians up to?*

Brown, R and J Meyer. *Antioch and Rome: New Testament Cradles of Christianity*. New York: Paulist Press, 1983.

Frend, W H C . *Saints and Sinners in the Early Church* (see above), Chapter 1.

Lienhard, J ed. *Ministry*. Message of the Fathers of the Church, no. 8. Wilmington, Delaware: Michael Glazier, 1984.

Staniforth, M ed. *Early Christian Writings*. Harmondsworth, Middlesex: Penguin, 1968.

Tugwell, S. *The Apostolic Fathers*. Outstanding Christian Thinkers Series. London: Geoffrey Chapman, 1989.

WEEK THREE *What did the pagans think?*

Barnes, T. 'Pagan Perceptions of Christianity' in Hazlett, ed. *Early Christianity*, pp 231–243.

Benko, S. *Pagan Rome and the Early Christians*. London: Batsford, 1985.

Dodds, E R. *Pagan and Christian in an Age of Anxiety*. Cambridge: Cambridge University Press, 1965.

Ferguson, E. *Backgrounds of Early Christianity*. Grand Rapids: Eerdmans, 1987.

Wilken, R L. *The Christians as the Romans Saw Them*. London and New Haven: Yale University Press, 1984.

WEEK FOUR *The government's reaction, and*
WEEK FIVE *The ultimate witness*

Frend, W H C. *Martyrdom and Persecution in the Early Church*. Oxford: Blackwell, 1965.

Frend, W H C. *The Rise of Christianity*, Chapters 9 and 13.

King, N. 'Church–State Relations' in Hazlett, ed. *Early Christianity*, pp 244–255.

Musurillo, E. *The Acts of the Christian Martyrs*. Oxford Early Christian Texts. Oxford: Oxford University Press, 1972.

WEEK SIX *Hellenistic culture*

Chadwick, H. *Early Christian Thought and the Classical Tradition*. Oxford: Oxford University Press, 1966.

Martin, L H. 'The Pagan Religious Background' in Hazlett, ed. *Early Christianity*, pp 52–64.

Stead, C. 'Greek Influence on Christian Thought' in *Early Christianity*, pp 175–185.

Walsh, M J. *A History of Philosophy*. London: Geoffrey Chapman, 1985.

WEEK SEVEN *Orthodoxy versus heresy*

Frend W H C. *Saints and Sinners in the Early Church*, Chapters 2 and 3.

Logan, A and J Wedderburn eds. *The New Testament and Gnosis.* Edinburgh: T & T Clark, 1983.

Pagels, E. *The Gnostic Gospels.* London: Weidenfeld & Nicolson, 1979.

Robinson, J M ed. *The Nag Hammadi Library in English.* New York: Harper & Row, 1977.

Rudolph, K. *Gnosis: The Nature and History of an Ancient Religion.* Edinburgh: T & T Clark, 1984.

Wiles, M. 'Orthodoxy and Heresy' in Hazlett, ed. *Early Christianity*, pp 198–207.

## WEEK EIGHT *The role of women*

Clarke, E A. *Women in the Early Church.* Message of the Fathers of the Church, no. 13. Wilmington, Delaware: Michael Glazier, 1983.

Heine, S. *Women in Early Christianity: Are the Feminist Scholars Right?* Translated by J Bowden. London: SCM, 1987.

Witherington III, B. *Women in the Earliest Churches.* Society for New Testament Studies Monograph Series 59. Cambridge: 1988.

## WEEK NINE *The triumph of Christianity?*

Greenslade, S L. *Church and State Relations From Constantine to Theodosius.* London: SCM, 1954.

Frend, W H C. *The Rise of Christianity*, Chapter 14.

Jones, A H. *Constantine and the Conversion of Europe.* New York: Macmillan, 1949.

Kee, A. *Constantine Versus Christ: The Triumph of Ideology.* London: SCM, 1982.

King, N. 'Church–State Relations' in Hazlett, ed. *Early Christianity*, pp 244–55.

## WEEK TEN *Christian attitudes to war and violence*

Swift, L. *The Early Fathers on War and Military Service.* Message of the Fathers of the Church, no. 19. Wilmington, Delaware: Michael Glazier, 1983.

## WEEK ELEVEN *Jesus Christ: God or godly?*

Chadwick, H. *The Early Church*, Chapters 8 and 9.

Fortman, E. *The Triune God: A Historical Study of the Doctrine of the Trinity*. Grand Rapids: Baker, 1972.

Gregg, R and D Groh. *Early Arianism: A View of Salvation*. London: SCM, 1981.

Kelly, J D. *Early Christian Doctrines*. 5th ed. London: A. & C. Black, 1977; New York: Harper & Row, 1978.

Rusch, W ed. *The Trinitarian Controversy*. Sources of Early Christian Thought. Philadelphia: Fortress Press, 1980.

Williams, R. *Arius: Heresy and Tradition*. London: Darton, Longman & Todd, 1987.

## WEEK TWELVE *More disputes*

Chadwick, H. *The Early Church*, Chapter 14.

Frend, W H C. *Saints and Sinners in the Early Church*, Chapter 7.

Norris, R ed. *The Christological Controversy*. Sources for Early Christian Thought. Philadelphia: Fortress Press, 1980.

Sellers, R. *The Council of Chalcedon: A Historical and Doctrinal Study*. London: SPCK, 1953.

Young, F. *From Nicaea to Chalcedon*. London: SCM, 1983.

## WEEK THIRTEEN *A great preacher*

Chadwick, H. *The Early Church*, Chapter 13.

Baur, C. *John Chrysostom and his Times*. 2 vols. London: Sands, 1959.

Gonzalez, J L. *Faith and Wealth: A History of Early Christian Ideas on the Origin, Significance, and Use of Money*. San Francisco: Harper & Row, 1990.

Phan, P C. *Social Thought*. Message of the Fathers of the Church, no. 20. Wilmington, Delaware: Michael Glazier, 1984.

Ramsey, B. 'Christian Attitudes to Poverty and Wealth' in Hazlett, ed. *Early Christianity*, pp 256–265.

WEEK FOURTEEN *The development of monasticism*

Athanasius. *The Life of Antony and the Letter to Marcellinus*. Translated by R C Gregg. Classics of Western Spirituality. London: SPCK, 1980.

Brown, P. *The World of Late Antiquity*. London: Thames & Hudson, 1971.

Brown, P. *Society and the Holy in Late Antiquity*. London: Faber, 1982.

Brown, P. *The Body and Society: Men, Women and Sexual Renunciation in Early Christianity*. London and Boston: Faber, 1989.

Chadwick, H. *The Early Church*, Chapter 12.

Knowles, D. *Christian Monasticism*. London: Weidenfeld & Nicolson, 1969.

*The Lives of the Desert Fathers*. Introduction by B Ward. Translated by N Russell. London and Oxford: Mowbray, 1980.

Rousseau, P. 'Christian Asceticism and the Early Monks' in Hazlett, ed. *Early Christianity*, pp 112–122.

WEEK FIFTEEN *Confessions*

St Augustine's *Confessions*. Various editions.